MANAGING PROJECT STAKEHOLDERS

MANAGING PROJECT

STAKEHOLDERS

BUILDING A FOUNDATION to ACHIEVE PROJECT GOALS

TRES ROEDER, MBA, PMP

WILEY

Published by John Wiley & Sons, Inc., Hoboken, New Jersey.
Published simultaneously in Canada.

Material from PMBOK® Guide, 5th ed., has been adapted and reproduced with the permission of PMI. Project Management Institute, A Guide to the Project Management Body of Knowledge (PMBOK® Guide)–Fifth Edition, Project Management Institute, Inc., 2012.

For general information on our other products and services or for technical support, please contact our Customer Care Department within the United States at (800) 762-2974, outside the United States at (317) 572-3993 or fax (317) 572-4002.

Wiley publishes in a variety of print and electronic formats and by print-on-demand. Some material included with standard print versions of this book may not be included in e-books or in print-on-demand. If this book refers to media such as a CD or DVD that is not included in the version you purchased, you may download this material at http://booksupport.wiley.com. For more information about Wiley products, visit www.wiley.com.

Library of Congress Cataloging-in-Publication Data:

Roeder, Tres, 1968–
    Managing Project Stakeholders/Tres Roeder, MBA, PMP.
      pages cm
    Includes bibliographical references and index.
    ISBN 978-1-118-50427-7 (cloth); ISBN 978-1-118-50428-4 (ePDF);
    ISBN 978-1-118-50426-0 (ePub); ISBN 978-1-118-50425-3 (Mobi)
      1. Project management. I. Title.
    HD69.P75.R64   2013
    658.4'04—dc23

                                                        2013001466

Printed in the United States of America

10 9 8 7 6 5 4 3 2 1

To Elizabeth, Parker, Garrett,
and man's best friend, Batman

The dogmas of the quiet past are inadequate to the stormy present. The occasion is piled high with difficulty, and we must rise with the occasion. As our case is new, so we must think anew and act anew.

—*Abraham Lincoln*

Contents

Foreword

Projects are done by people (the team) and for people (the stakeholders). While tools, techniques, and technologies are certainly important, the people's participation and perception about the project and its deliverables is really what makes or breaks a project. As such, the project's success is ultimately defined by stakeholders, and in particular by the beneficiaries of the project's outcome(s); they can consider a project successful if the deliverables truly meet their needs, even if the project's execution may not perfectly fit within the traditional triple constraint of "full scope, in time, within budget."

As this concept is embraced more and more by the project management community it has resulted in increased focus on stakeholder management as a critical component of project management, beyond the traditional Communications Management knowledge area. This trend was recently recognized in arguably the most widespread standard in the area, *A Guide to Project Management Body of Knowledge* (PMBOK® Guide), 5th ed., published by Project Management Institute (PMI), by introducing a new knowledge area dedicated to project stakeholder management.

In terms of full disclosure, the author of this Foreword was part of the core team for the *PMBOK® Guide* – 5th ed., and coordinated the teams working in the "soft skills" areas of the standard—the knowledge areas for human resources, communication, and the newly introduced stakeholder management. Introducing the new knowledge area was confirmation that this is indeed a best practice "for most project managers, in most projects, most of the time."

In the above capacity, I had the opportunity to interact with a group of dedicated, top-level professionals that participated in the editing teams, and discuss their experiences around the world in stakeholder management, as well as the results of various studies and research in the area. It demonstrated beyond any doubt the importance and extent of actively managing stakeholder participation in projects not only for a successful project execution, but also for the ultimate use of project's deliverables to meet the organizational needs that triggered the project in the first place.

Tres Roeder, the author of this book, is a long-time champion of the stakeholder management domain and a public advocate of its importance for project managers. He is a globally recognized project management expert, invited to share his expertise not only as a consultant for many top-level organizations, but also as an applauded speaker at international conferences and other public events. Through his articles, seminars, webinars, courses, workshops, and blogs Mr. Roeder combines hands-on experience corralling high performing stakeholder teams with the latest research in the area to promote formal, sustained, and efficient stakeholder management as one of the main enablers of achieving project success.

In his first book, A *Sixth Sense for Project Management*, Mr. Roeder detailed how to achieve project success by deploying a balanced approach with a particular emphasis on people. His interest in the domain continues with the present book focused on stakeholder management. With a particular insight gained by acting as a reviewer of the draft project stakeholder management knowledge area introduced in *PMBOK®* *Guide* – 5th ed., Tres Roeder brings in his extensive expertise in the area to complement, detail, and explain various components of this evolving domain.

Unlike other works in the area, this book brings a new perspective by incorporating "technical project management skills" (formulas, frameworks, tools, etc.) into a "soft skills" area such as stakeholders' management to add consistency, repeatability, and predictability to a domain that is variable, unique, and volatile by definition. It provides the reader with the necessary knowledge and practical examples to be able to understand, classify, and manage basically any stakeholders that may be encountered in real-life projects.

The book is structured in four sections, each including three chapters, which progressively build up the reader's understanding of stakeholders' management.

Section One discusses fundamental concepts for successful project stakeholder management. The introductory chapter defines project stakeholders as people who are subject to, part of, or have decision-making over a project, followed by two chapters dedicated to techniques to categorize project stakeholders and creating a prioritization strategy for project stakeholders.

Section Two discusses five stakeholder groups: project team stakeholders, executive stakeholders, external stakeholders, stakeholders subject to the changes, and phantom stakeholders. The chapters included in Section Two provide a detailed discussion of Project Team Stakeholders and Executive Stakeholders, and considerations about the remaining groups in the chapter Other Stakeholders.

Section Three focuses on managing stakeholder communication with special consideration being given to projects that take place in a virtual environment. The section concludes with practical advice on handling project conflicts that could occur with difficult stakeholders.

Section Four complements the specific project management skills with general management competencies that the project manager can deploy in all kinds of situations. The capabilities treated in the last section of the book are leadership, obtaining buy in, and negotiation.

This book contains not only a formal treatment of essential topics for successful stakeholder management, but also many high-impact tips project managers should know and be able to apply in order to effectively engage stakeholders in project execution, and secure their support to ensure a project's success. It is an indispensable reading for every project manager that aspires to get beyond the technicalities of "percent complete" and move into leading projects that all stakeholders will consider successful.

George Jucan, MSc PMP

Preface

Managing *Project Stakeholders* is intended for anyone who works with people to accomplish project results. Historically, project management literature has focused on the technical skills required to document, track, and quantify projects. Although important, these technical skills correlate less to project success than the real world interpersonal skills addressed in this book. The successful project manager must know how to work with different types of people.

This book can be read from beginning to end for an advanced understanding of working with project stakeholders. Alternatively, the busy professional can jump directly into the section or chapter most relevant to them. Each chapter is written as a free-standing module. Where there are connections to previous or subsequent chapters it will be noted in the text.

Section One creates the foundation for successful project stakeholder management. The section is divided into three chapters: What Is a Stakeholder, Categorizing Stakeholders, and Prioritizing Stakeholders.

In Chapter 1, What Is a Stakeholder?, we define project stakeholders as people who are subject to, are part of, or have decision making over a project. We discuss how project stakeholder management is most successful when it fits into a holistic and balanced approach to managing projects and managing change that includes technical project management skills, business acumen, and interpersonal skills.

In Chapter 2, Categorizing Stakeholders, we share techniques to categorize project stakeholders. We develop a common language to use when describing stakeholders. As a profession, a common language helps us work more efficiently and more seamlessly across organizations and industries.

In Chapter 3, Prioritizing Stakeholders, we use the categorization techniques from Chapter 2 to create a prioritization strategy for project stakeholders. Project managers must carefully deploy their time. Using thoughtful two-by-two matrices, Chapter 3 instructs us how to identify the most important stakeholders without losing focus on the other stakeholders.

Section Two discusses five stakeholder groups: project team stakeholders, executive stakeholders, external stakeholders, stakeholders subject to the change, and phantom stakeholders. Stakeholders in each group may have much in common with one another. Section Two is divided into three chapters: Project Team Members, Executive Stakeholders, and Other Stakeholders.

Chapter 4, Project Team Members, discusses techniques to manage the project team. Project managers are likely to spend most of their time working with project team stakeholders. Chapter 4 discusses how to kick off the project team, build relationships within the team, and create an environment that is poised for success.

Chapter 5, Executive Stakeholders, focuses on working collaboratively with the executives directing the project. In many cases the executive stakeholders are the single most powerful stakeholder group. In this chapter the project manager will learn techniques to harness the power of executive stakeholders to the benefit of the project team.

Chapter 6, Other Stakeholders, explains three additional stakeholder groups: external stakeholders, stakeholders subject to the change, and phantom stakeholders. The project manager will learn how to work with each of these groups to increase the probability of project success.

Section Three focuses on project communication and conflict. The section is divided into three chapters: Stakeholder Communication, Managing Stakeholders in a Virtual World, and Managing Difficult Stakeholders.

In Chapter 7, Stakeholder Communication, we focus on different paths to communication success. The successful project manager communicates messages that are clear, consistent, and frequently repeated through multiple communication channels.

In Chapter 8, Managing Stakeholders in a Virtual World, we discuss an area of growing importance, how to work with remotely located stakeholders. Stakeholder management in virtual environments has similarities to and important differences from the in-person environment.

In Chapter 9, Managing Difficult Stakeholders, we discuss techniques for working with stakeholders who present challenges to the project team. Despite the project manager's best efforts, there may still be certain stakeholders who have a different perspective on the project. Chapter 9 presents real-world solutions to dealing with these individuals.

Section Four provides a portfolio of general management skills the project manager can deploy in all types of situations. The section is divided into three chapters: Leadership, Buy-In, and Negotiation.

Chapter 10, Leadership, begins with the premise that all project managers are leaders. Project stakeholders look to the project manager to provide guidance and direction. Chapter 10 provides a situational leadership framework based on A Sixth Sense for Project Management®.

Chapter 11, Buy-In, offers a three-step process for use to gain support. Project stakeholders have a variety of perspectives, attitudes, and beliefs. The Buy-In chapter contains a powerful framework that can be adapted to earn the support of each project stakeholder.

Chapter 12, Negotiation, provides 10 high-impact tips the project manager can deploy to succeed in project negotiations. Projects are a constant negotiation, whether about resources for the project, the time line, or the scope. In this chapter project managers will learn how to get what they need for project success.

Acknowledgments

I offer deep gratitude to my family for providing ongoing encouragement and support for this project. To my wife Elizabeth for her love and behind-the-scenes support; to my son Parker, who showed a keen interest for every step in the writing process; to my son Garrett for the late-night chats; and to our dog Batman, who spent many (not so) tough days lying at my side chewing on a bone while I typed.

Thanks to George Jucan, PMP®, for his leadership overseeing the team that wrote Chapter 13 on project stakeholder management in the *PMBOK® Guide*, 5th ed., and to all those on the team who wrote this important work. I am honored and thankful to have George's insight captured in the Foreword to this book.

I owe much to the dedicated team at Roeder Consulting who kept the lights on while I focused on writing. In particular, thanks to Keith Jenkins, Jim Kups, and Sarah Nicol.

Thanks to Rob Mansfield, firefighter with Squad 2 in the Chicago Fire Department, and Lt. Anthony Carusso, Pepper Pike Fire Department, for fact-checking the fire crew examples in Chapter 10 on

Leadership. Putting out a fire literally is a project that has many lessons for the figurative fires the rest of us put out every day.

I would like to thank Kelley Management Consulting for mentoring me and teaching me much about aligning people around a common goal in the fast-paced environment of organizational change. In particular, thanks to Patrick Kelley, Jim Schumann, and Erich Weber.

I am thankful for the world-class team at John Wiley & Sons for supporting and executing this project. Thanks to Debra Englander for believing in the concept, Jennifer MacDonald and Donna Martone for overseeing editing and document creation, and Tula Batanchiev for expert marketing.

As always, thanks to all of you who attend Roeder Consulting's courses, trust us with a consulting or training project, or are otherwise connected to the Roeder Consulting family. I learn from you every day and treasure your friendship and support.

T.R.

Section One

STAKEHOLDER MANAGEMENT OVERVIEW

S ection One creates the foundation for successful project stakeholder management. The section is divided into three chapters: What Is a Stakeholder?, Categorizing Stakeholders, and Prioritizing Stakeholders.

In Chapter 1, What Is a Stakeholder?, we define project stakeholders as people who are subject to, are part of, or have decision making over a project. We discuss how project stakeholder management is most successful when it fits into a holistic and balanced approach to managing projects and managing change that includes technical project management skills, business acumen, and interpersonal skills.

In Chapter 2, Categorizing Stakeholders, we share techniques to categorize project stakeholders. We develop a common language to use when describing stakeholders. As a profession, a common language helps us work more efficiently and more seamlessly across organizations and industries.

In Chapter 3, Prioritizing Stakeholders, we use the categorization techniques from Chapter 2 to create a prioritization strategy for project stakeholders. Project managers must carefully deploy their time. Using simple two-by-two matrices, Chapter 3 instructs us how to identify the most important stakeholders without losing focus on the other stakeholders.

Chapter One

What Is a Stakeholder?

It is never too late to be what you might have been.
George Eliot

Projects require people. People are needed to conceive the idea for the project, design project plans, approve the plans, execute the plans, and close out the project. People are impacted by the outcome of the project. Whether the project is implementing a new software system, a new business unit, or a new bridge, there will be an impact on people. All of these people are stakeholders.

Project Managers Must Be Nimble

This book discusses how to effectively identify, categorize, prioritize, manage, and lead project stakeholders. Projects are temporary endeavors, so project managers must learn how to launch a team of stakeholders, manage the team for the duration of the project, then thank and disband the team when the project is complete. This stands in contrast to operational management, which is more permanent in nature.

Project management is a discipline focused on delivering results and then moving on to the next project. In contrast to operational management, projects have a defined beginning point and a defined end point. Operational management is focused on the tasks and activities required to manage an organization on an ongoing basis.

The temporary nature of projects leads to transient stakeholders. Project stakeholders come and go as the project works through different phases. When the project ends, the stakeholder group is disbanded. Operational management, in contrast, may focus on the same stakeholders for years. An occasional stakeholder may come or go, but the overall stakeholder base is far less transient in operational management than in project management. As a result, project managers must be nimble, adaptable, and constantly vigilant to understand their stakeholder environment.

The Balanced Approach

Project stakeholder management requires a robust skill set. Effective project managers must have expert knowledge of their project scope and plans. They must know what they are trying to do and the constraints upon them to get it done. And they must be able to work with people. Successful project managers deploy a three-pronged approach to managing their projects: technical project management skills, business acumen, and "sixth sense" people skills. (See Figure 1.1.)

Technical Skills

Technical project management skills are the formulas, frameworks, and processes of project management. Technical skills include earned value management, writing a charter, creating a work breakdown structure (WBS), and so on. When we use the term *technical skills* in this book we are *not* referring to knowledge of the underlying technologies, products, or services the project is developing. Expertise in the underlying product technology is not necessarily required for successful project managers. What is required, however, is expertise in the technical skills and frameworks used to manage projects. Successful project

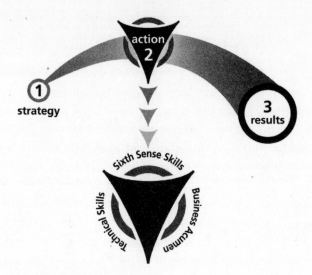

Figure 1.1 The Balanced Approach

managers understand these technical skills and know when to deploy them to facilitate project success. They also know when the standard technical skills are not appropriate and adapt accordingly.

Business Acumen

Business acumen is knowledge of the organization's goals, strategies, and language. Business acumen is understanding how one's project will help the organization achieve its goals and strategies. Effective project managers understand *why* the project is important. At any point in the project life cycle effective project managers can describe not only what they're doing but also why they're doing it and why it matters to the organization. This is business acumen.

The successful project manager also understands the operational and strategic language of the organization. The project manager should know terms such as *return on investment*, *net present value*, and *strategic alignment*. Each organization has its own unique language to describe strategic goals and the tactics deployed to achieve the goals. It is important for the project manager to understand and use this language.

Importance of Business Acumen

Many organizations deploy a Project Management Office (PMO) to oversee major projects. Interestingly, the number of organizations with PMOs is declining and many of those still having PMOs are reducing the staff in them. Recent research from The Hackett Group shows that there may be good reason for the decline. On average, PMOs increase the cost of an organization's information technology (IT) function without delivering improvement to the on-time or on-budget performance of projects.

There's an interesting twist, however. Top performing IT organizations continue to use PMOs and get results from them. Business acumen is one of the key factors correlated to successful PMOs in these top performers. Successful PMOs hold their project teams accountable for business results.

SOURCE: "Most Companies with Project Management Offices See Higher IT Costs, No Performance Improvements," The Hackett Group, November 1, 2012.

"Sixth Sense" People Skills

Third, and most importantly, effective project managers know how to work with people to achieve results. They are strong communicators, good negotiators, effective leaders, and astute observers of human behavior. Decades of research proves that people skills are the most important driver of effective project management. The project manager's ability to harness their expertise and intuition to lead people to successful outcomes is called "A Sixth Sense for Project Management®."

Together, the three core capabilities of technical skills, business acumen, and people skills comprise the Balanced Approach. Alone, each of these skills is not enough. Together, they form a powerful method for change. Successful project stakeholder management requires the Balanced Approach.

A Sixth Sense for Project Management®

The first section in the book *A Sixth Sense for Project Management* highlights the need for the project management profession to embrace people skills. Section One, comprised of three chapters, documents research showing that people skills are more highly correlated with project success than project management technical skills.

At the conclusion of Section One project managers are asked to come together to broadcast the message that interpersonal skills are critically important. Others in the profession are champions of people skills, too. The message has been heard; the latest version of the *PMBOK® Guide* includes a chapter devoted to stakeholder management, Chapter 13.

There's still much work to do. Many project managers and project organizations continue to have an unhealthy overemphasis on the technical side of project and change management. Working together, we must continue to strive toward the more balanced approach that has proven to greatly increase the probability of project success.

The Project Management Institute

The Project Management Institute (PMI) is a not-for-profit global project management association. Founded in 1969, PMI has grown from humble beginnings to a powerhouse with almost a half-million people globally holding its foundational professional designation, the Project Management Professional (PMP®).

The Project Management Body of Knowledge (PMBOK® Guide)

PMI correctly recognized that the profession of project management did not have a common knowledge base. In the past, when a group of project managers got together they did not have common terminology to describe what they were doing. They might take a large part of their meeting figuring out what the others were talking about. Recognizing this gap PMI commissioned a project to create a global standard. The goal was a standard that could be used in almost any project situation. After a number of years of effort the first standard was published in 1987. The standard was named *A Guide to the Project Management Body of Knowledge*. Today, in its fifth edition, we will call this document the *PMBOK®️ Guide*.

PMBOK®️ Guide, Chapter 13

For the first time, the *PMBOK®️ Guide* includes a chapter on project stakeholder management. Chapter 13, Project Stakeholder Management, is one of the 10 knowledge areas. Each of the knowledge areas represents foundational information all project managers must know. Adding project stakeholder management to the knowledge areas is a major and game-changing development.

Increased Emphasis on People Skills   Chapter 13 is game-changing for several reasons. First, it is the most attention authors of the *PMBOK®️ Guide* have devoted to project stakeholders. Stakeholders have always been critical to project success. Regrettably, these skills have not been a major part of a project manager's professional development requirements until recently. Many project managers and organizations incorrectly view project management as a skill mainly focused on technical skills. People and organizations with this misguided understanding are more likely to suffer from failed projects.

People Skills Integrated into Technical Skills   A second reason why Chapter 13 is game-changing is because its addition to the *PMBOK®️ Guide* demonstrates that stakeholder management is integrated into the technical skills required to manage projects. For example, one of the key documents in Chapter 13 is the "Stakeholder Register." The stakeholder register is a form that must be completed to document and

Researching the Value of Project Management

"Researching the Value of Project Management" is a multiyear, multimillion-dollar project sponsored by the Project Management Institute. The goal is to answer the question "Does project management deliver value?" and if it does, "What are the key drivers of value?" Not surprisingly, the study did indeed find that project management delivers value.

However, the study also found that project management does not *always* deliver value. In some cases, project management makes things worse. Project managers make things worse when they do not deploy awareness of the situation to adapt their project management approach and techniques. The study tracked a number of variables and determined which variables, if any, are correlated to project success. Many variables that were investigated, including a number of technical project management skills, did not correlate to project success. Leadership, interpersonal skills, and the project manager's ability to read the project situation and adapt did correlate to project success.

SOURCE: Mark Mullaly and Janice Thompson, *Researching the Value of Project Management* (Newtown Square, PA: Project Management Institute, 2008).

categorize project stakeholders. Other knowledge areas of the *PMBOK®️ Guide* have tools and techniques that are inputs into the stakeholder register. The stakeholder register itself is an input into knowledge areas such as project risk management and project human resources management. In simple language, this means that project stakeholder management is a technical project management skill in addition to an interpersonal skill. Project stakeholder management is integrated into the technical process of project management.

See Chapter 3, Prioritizing Stakeholders, for more detail on the stakeholder register.

Holistic Approach to Project Management A third reason why Chapter 13 is game-changing is that it highlights the concept of a holistic approach to project management. As discussed previously, this is called the Balanced Approach. Chapter 13 merges interpersonal skills, technical skills, and, to a more limited extent, business acumen into the required and standardized language of PMP®s. This is a major step toward improving project success rates. As a profession, we fail more often than we succeed. A primary reason for this failure is an overreliance on only one of the three types of skills required in the Balanced Approach— technical project management skills. The skills project managers most often use as a crutch are the technical skills. We must embrace the Balanced Approach if we are to improve project success rates. Chapter 13 in the *PMBOK® Guide* is a solid step in the right direction.

Disclosure

The author served as a subject matter expert reviewer of the *PMBOK® Guide*'s new chapter on project stakeholder management, Chapter 13. One of several individuals selected globally to preview the chapter before final release, the author reviewed a draft version of Chapter 13 and provided feedback in 2011. A number of the author's recommendations were integrated into the final text for Chapter 13.

PMBOK® Guide, Appendix G

The prior version of the *PMBOK Guide* (the fourth edition) includes a brief appendix, Appendix G, which mentions interpersonal skills. Appendix G is about six pages long and served the purpose of putting project managers on notice that there is more to their craft than the technical skills they learned in the preceding 400+ pages of the fourth edition. With Appendix G in the fourth edition and Chapter 13 and an appendix on interpersonal skills in the fifth edition, we are seeing the project management establishment move further toward embracing the importance of the human side of project management.

Stakeholder Defined

Project managers did not previously have a common definition for project stakeholders. With the introduction of Chapter 13 in the *PMBOK®Guide*, we now have a common definition to use. The *PMBOK® Guide* defines a project stakeholder as follows:

> An individual, group, or organization who may affect, be affected by, or perceive itself to be affected by a decision, activity, or outcome of a project.

In the following section we discuss this definition in more detail.

A Stakeholder Is an Individual, Group, or Organization

Project stakeholders may represent themselves, a group, or an organization. The project manager's approach to managing each stakeholder varies according to which of these categories the stakeholder fits into.

Individuals representing themselves do not need to communicate with others in their constituency to develop consensus. They *are* the constituency. Groups and organizations, however, may have one person who is the main stakeholder representing the group or a combination of stakeholders each of whom must be dealt with individually. The effective project manager understands the level of authority each stakeholder has and reacts accordingly. (See Table 1.1.)

See Section Two, Stakeholder Groups, for details on each stakeholder group.

Table 1.1 Individuals, Groups, and Organizations

	Individual	**Group**	**Organization**
Definition	A single stakeholder	Two or more stakeholders with a common affiliation, such as serving in the same functional area or working in the same product group	A combination of two or more groups
Competing interests	None	Multiple	Multiple
Lines of communication	One	Multiple—communicate with each person in the group	Multiple and complex—communicate with each person in each group and also across groups

A Stakeholder May Affect

Stakeholders have the option to make a difference. Anyone who can or does make a difference in a project is a stakeholder. There are numerous ways a stakeholder can affect a project. A few examples are:

- Conceive the idea for the project.
- Initiate the project.
- Set and/or approve the project budget.
- Provide input into project scope.
- Plan the project.
- Approve the project.
- Participate on the project team.
- Publicly support or resist the project.
- Rally a group to support or resist the project.

This broad definition of project stakeholders is likely to result in a large group of people. Many project managers may be surprised at how large their list of stakeholders becomes when they adopt the definition of stakeholders used in the *PMBOK® Guide*. One of the implications of a larger list of stakeholders is that project managers will need to improve their ability to strategically deploy their time across stakeholders and stakeholder groups.

See Chapter 3, Prioritizing Stakeholders, for details on how project managers can strategically deploy their time across stakeholders.

A Stakeholder May Be Affected By

Stakeholders in the previous section were either actively involved in the project or had the choice of becoming actively involved. These stakeholders could affect the project. In this next section of the definition we cast the net more broadly to anyone who might be affected by the project. These people may or may not be able to influence the project. Ideally, we want all stakeholders who are going to be affected by a project to have input into the process. Realistically, in many projects this is not feasible.

Stakeholders May Perceive Themselves to Be Affected By

The next group of stakeholders defined in the *PMBOK® Guide* are those who perceive themselves to be affected by the project. The concept is that perception is reality. If people think they are stakeholders then they are going to act in ways that they think a stakeholder might act. For example, they might attend project meetings. They might provide feedback on project documents. They might attempt to change the scope of the project. The definition of a stakeholder in the *PMBOK® Guide*'s Chapter 13 argues that this person, by definition, is a stakeholder.

Indeed, the project manager will need to manage the situation when people think they are stakeholders. Whether it's by diplomatically asking them not to attend team meetings or by deciding to incorporate them into the project, the project manager will use project stakeholder management tools and techniques to manage the situation.

A Decision, Activity, or Outcome of a Project

Stakeholders sometimes are decision makers. In other cases they do not have any decision-making authority. Stakeholders may have the ability to influence decisions others make. Influence can come in the form of

How Do You Manage Individuals Who Perceive Themselves to Be Stakeholders?

This topic has led to interesting conversation in public classes on advanced project stakeholder management. Some project managers argue that they should not be responsible for people who perceive themselves to be stakeholders but who are not actually stakeholders. These people are an annoyance, the argument goes, and just one more problem the project manager must deal with. Calling them a stakeholder indicates, they say, that anyone can force their way into the project. The project manager loses control.

Other project managers think of stakeholders more broadly. They consider this group who perceives themselves to be stakeholders as an important faction that must be managed.

The answer comes down to how we define stakeholders. If stakeholders are defined as only the people *we want* to be on the project, then an individual who perceives himself or herself as a stakeholder is not one. However, if we think of stakeholders more broadly, as defined in the *PMBOK® Guide*, then these people become stakeholders.

Steps the project manager goes through to categorize and manage people who perceive themselves to be stakeholders are likely to be the same as the steps for those who are officially on the list. Therefore, individuals who perceive themselves to be stakeholders should be considered stakeholders for the purposes of tracking, categorizing, and managing them.

See Chapter 6, Other Stakeholders, for details on phantom stakeholders who act as stakeholders but are unrecognized as stakeholders by the project manager or the project team.

research, data, opinions, a persuasive argument, or other means such as bringing together a group of like-minded individuals and representing their cause.

Stakeholders might be involved with the entire project or just one aspect of the project. The activities they touch will vary. The savvy project manager understands that the stakeholders are not a single homogeneous group of people with the same interests. Instead, stakeholders are unique individuals with their own sets of interests, fears, and aspirations.

Our Working Definition of a Stakeholder

For purposes of this book, we will simplify the definition of a stakeholder to the following: people who are subject to, are part of, or have decision making over a project.

This definition captures the essence of the *PMBOK® Guide* definition but is simpler and uses fewer words. In general, anyone involved in the project in any manner is considered a stakeholder.

Stakeholder Management across Methodologies

The *PMBOK® Guide* focuses on the waterfall method of project management. In the waterfall method the project flows in phases from initiating, to planning, to executing, to monitoring and controlling, and finally to closing. Each phase, in theory, flows into the next. Project managers using the waterfall method will find that the concepts discussed in this book will apply directly to their projects.

The concepts in this book, however, are not exclusive to the waterfall method. The fundamentals of stakeholder management, as discussed in this book, are equally relevant to agile, lean, and other forms of project management.

Further, business analysts will find value in the pages of this book. As a business analyst goes through the work of capturing business requirements and gaining consensus, stakeholder management will be a core skill for success.

See Section Three, Stakeholder Communication and Conflict, and Section Four, General Stakeholder Management Skills, for more detail on the general skills required to manage stakeholders in any situation.

Stakeholder Management Is Universal

Project stakeholder management is about people. People are involved in all projects. This is true regardless of the project management methodology used. There are many different technical project management methodologies, including waterfall, agile, extreme, and lean. The tools and techniques discussed in this book can be applied to any form of project management and change management.

Also, stakeholder management tools and techniques can be used in organizations of all sizes, across different industries, in organizations with different types of cultures, and so on. What is different, however, is the specific way the tools and techniques are deployed. No two project environments are the same so savvy project managers understand how to adapt their stakeholder management tools and techniques to the specific environment their project is operating in.

Stakeholder Management Is Like a Game of Golf

Golfers use almost exactly the same bag of clubs on all different types of golf courses. However, the details of each shot are different depending on what type of material the ball is resting on, the wind conditions, whether the hole is above or below the golf ball, and so on.

Think of the bag of clubs as the project manager's stakeholder management tools and techniques. Think of each project as a different golf course. The way the tools and techniques are applied will change based on a variety of conditions that will be discussed in this book.

Summary

In summary, stakeholder management is required for all types of projects and change management processes. The tools and skills developed in the discipline of stakeholder management cut across all project management frameworks. The ability to identify, mobilize, motivate, and lead stakeholders will always be in demand for the individuals who lead change.

The discipline of stakeholder management is essential to project success. As part of the Balanced Approach, the successful project manager is an expert on managing the people in the project and harnessing their energy to achieve the desired project goals.

We defined stakeholders as "people who are subject to, are part of, or have decision making over a project." Building on this definition, we will assign stakeholders into groups, categorize and prioritize stakeholders, and discuss how to communicate to and lead stakeholders.

A project may have many different stakeholders, all bringing their own unique needs and desires. Without proper management techniques, this can become overwhelming for the project manager. The first technique we will discuss is how to categorize stakeholders to bring clarity and understanding to the fog of project implementation. This is the topic of the next chapter, Categorizing Stakeholders.

Chapter Two

Categorizing Stakeholders

All stakeholders are equal, but some are more equal than others.
Paraphrased from George Orwell, Animal Farm

I t is self-evident that stakeholders are not all the same. The project manager must have a common language to use for categorizing the different stakeholders. In this chapter we discuss common terminology that can be used to describe and categorize project stakeholders.

The project manager also requires documents to track stakeholders. In this chapter we introduce two documents to capture project stakeholder information: the stakeholder engagement assessment matrix and the stakeholder management plan. These documents will be integrated into the next chapter when we discuss the stakeholder register.

We begin by discussing the importance of categorizing stakeholders. Categorizing stakeholders helps us develop our stakeholder management strategy related to three areas:

1. How much time to spend with each stakeholder.
2. The most important issues for each stakeholder.
3. The level of importance of each stakeholder's concerns.

Each is discussed in more detail in the following pages.

Benefits of Categorizing

Categorizing enables the project manager to strategically manage stakeholders. Each stakeholder offers a unique mix of knowledge, experience, opinions, and behaviors. A one-size-fits-all approach does not work. The successful project manager must create a framework to simplify the wide array of stakeholders into understandable and actionable categories.

How Much Time to Invest

Project managers are pulled in many different directions. They typically manage project scope, time line, cost, and other attributes while simultaneously managing stakeholders. The project manager must decide how much time to invest in each of these activities. This chapter and the next chapter on prioritization offer tools that help project managers determine how to allocate their time across the myriad of project stakeholders.

What Issues Are Most Important?

It is common in a project for there to be a small number of key issues or changes that lead to the most debate and discussion. Categorizing stakeholders by their level of passion for each of these issues may be helpful to the project manager. Communications and stakeholder management strategies can be targeted by issue group.

When the project manager discovers a block of multiple stakeholders who believe that a particular issue is most important, then the project manager can target issue-specific communications to this group. In contrast to one-on-one communications with each stakeholder, "issue group" focused communications are a more efficient way for the project manager to share information.

Relative Importance of Stakeholder Concerns

The project manager should prioritize stakeholders based on the potential impact of their concern on the project. Some concerns have more potential impact to the project than others. Stakeholders have a multitude of objections, concerns, and ideas about projects. The project manager must determine which objections carry real importance and which are frivolous.

In the absence of a strategy to prioritize stakeholder concerns the loudest voices are likely to get the most attention from the project manager and the project team. This is suboptimal, particularly in situations where the loudest voice is championing an issue that is relatively unimportant.

Relative Importance

Two stakeholders disagree about the plan for an office expansion project. In the project the current marketing department will be torn down and rebuilt into a more friendly work environment with open work spaces and environmentally friendly lighting.

Carlos, the first stakeholder, is concerned that the project will exceed the allocated budget. He cites similar projects that have been done in the past and all have gone over budget. He is arguing for a 10 percent contingency to be added to the project budget.

Carmen, the second stakeholder, has a different concern. She likes having a drinking fountain next to her desk. The construction team's current plans would move the drinking fountain into a shared lunchroom area that is 50 yards away from her.

Looking at the two concerns, the project manager can reasonably conclude that the first issue is more serious than the second. The project manager should spend more time looking into the budget and Carlos's argument. Carmen, in contrast, may be best managed with a single courtesy meeting to hear out her concerns. She may have valid reasons that should be incorporated into plans, or the conversation may show her concerns to be insignificant when compared to the concerns of other stakeholders.

Dimensions of Categorization

Let's discuss the different dimensions used to categorize stakeholders based on definitions in the *PMBOK® Guide*, 5th ed. We use terms from the *PMBOK® Guide* to help create a common language for discussing project stakeholders. In the next chapter we will build on these terms as we deepen our understanding of how to categorize and prioritize stakeholders.

A Note on Standard Terminology

One of the primary benefits of the *PMBOK® Guide* is to create a common language for the project management profession. The Project Management Institute, as discussed in Chapter 1, published the first guidelines in 1987. It provided a standard language for project managers. Prior to these first guidelines, project managers used different terms to describe the same concepts.

A document that one project manager called a charter another might call a kickoff document. This variation still exists today to a certain extent; each organization might have its own unique language. However, on the technical side of project management, the *PMBOK® Guide* has been a useful tool to provide a common language and a common set of tools and techniques for project managers.

The fifth edition of the *PMBOK® Guide*, published in January 2013, includes more detail than ever about the human side of project management. The fifth edition includes a new chapter on project stakeholder management, Chapter 13.

In the fifth edition we now see the initial drafts of a common language that project managers can use to describe stakeholders. We will be able to say to one another, "This stakeholder has a lot of interest," and we'll know exactly what that means. Like any standard, it is not perfect. Each of us may define some of these words differently than the *PMBOK® Guide* does. The project management profession, however, will benefit from understanding and using standard terminology.

Not only will this help project managers communicate with other project managers in their organization, but it will also make the project manager's skills more transferable across organizations. In an era when most people no longer enjoy so-called cradle-to-grave employment where they have the same job their entire career, it is in the best interest of both the employer and the project manager for the project manager to have transferable skills.

The employer benefits because it can hire project managers and feel confident they will know the appropriate language. Employers may also see improved communication between vendors and their organization as the project stakeholders adopt a common terminology.

Employees benefit, too, from having transferable skills. If their current employer decides their particular skills are no longer needed, or they move to a new city or change organizations, then they can more easily integrate into a new organization if they have transferable skills, including a common language for project stakeholders. Many organizations are unsure how to handle the project management function, and this creates some churn in project management roles and employment opportunities. Clearly, it is in the project managers' best interest to remain knowledgeable and relevant to their organization as well as to others should they find themselves out of work.

Therefore, as we discuss project stakeholder management in this chapter, when possible we will use the definitions of words as defined in the *PMBOK® Guide*. This will give all of us a common language to describe stakeholders.

Power

Power is the measure of a stakeholder's level of authority. Level of authority refers to the stakeholder's overall organizational power. Senior executives, by this definition, are likely to have significant power. Power, however, is not a measure of the stakeholder's ability to affect the particular project. There is a different word for this: *impact*.

Impact

Impact is a stakeholder's ability to effect changes to the project's planning or execution. A stakeholder with high impact can direct the project in their desired direction. It is possible for a stakeholder to have low power but high impact, and vice versa. See the inset for more detail.

Power versus Impact

The *PMBOK® Guide* creates unique definitions for the words *power* and *impact*. The *PMBOK® Guide* defines power as the "level of authority" of an individual. It defines impact as the stakeholder's "ability to effect changes to the project's planning or execution." Therefore, the words *power* and *impact* mean different things. For the benefit of standardization for our profession, when we use these words in this chapter we will use them consistently with how they are defined in the *PMBOK® Guide*.

It is important to note that power, as defined in the *PMBOK® Guide*, refers to overall organizational power. Therefore, power is the measure of a stakeholder's overall level of authority in the organization.

This does not necessarily translate into power to influence the project. Impact is the measure of the stakeholder's ability to bring about changes specifically on the project. Said differently, power is the ability to impose one's will across an organization, and impact is the ability to impose one's will on the specific project.

A high-power individual may have limited impact on a project if the project is outside of that person's area of responsibility. Conversely, a stakeholder with significant impact on a project, such as a subject matter expert, may hold very little power in the organization.

Table 2.1 Stakeholder Engagement Assessment Matrix

Stakeholder Name	Unaware	Resistant	Neutral	Supportive	Leading
Stakeholder	C			D	
Stakeholder			C	D	
Stakeholder				D C	

Source: Adapted from *PMBOK® Guide*, 5th ed.

Interest

Interest is a stakeholder's level of concern regarding the project outcomes. A stakeholder with high interest is very concerned about the project. A stakeholder with low interest, however, has other priorities that are more important than the outcomes of this particular project.

Influence

Influence is the stakeholder's level of active involvement in the project. A stakeholder with a high level of influence will participate more frequently in team discussions, meetings, and so on. A stakeholder with a low level of influence is not likely to participate in most team meetings.

Stakeholder Engagement Assessment Matrix

The stakeholder engagement assessment matrix helps the project manager categorize the current and desired attitudes of stakeholders. The matrix has five categories for attitudes: unsure, resistant, neutral, supportive, and leading. (See Table 2.1.)

Fields in the Stakeholder Engagement Assessment Matrix

The project manager should complete the fields in the matrix as follows:

- *Stakeholder name.* Enter the stakeholder's name or initials (or other identifier if confidentiality is desired).

- *Stakeholder's level of support.* Identify which of the following categories best describes the stakeholder:
  - Unsure—not knowledgeable on the project.
  - Resistant—opposed to the project.
  - Neutral—neither resistant nor supportive.
  - Supportive—in agreement with the project.
  - Leading—actively supporting the project.
- Time frame:
  - C—current state of the stakeholder.
  - D—desired state of the stakeholder.

See Chapter 11, Buy-In, for details on how to work with people who are unsure, resistant, neutral, supportive, and leading.

A brief glance at the stakeholder engagement assessment matrix shows project managers how much support they have. Also, it shows which stakeholders they need to work with. Any stakeholder with a desired state in a different column than the current state requires the project manager's attention. A stakeholder with a current state in the desired category, however, should not be taken for granted. The project manager should continue to include this stakeholder in the process and ensure that the proper support is maintained.

Sensitivity of Stakeholder Information

Information included in the stakeholder engagement assessment matrix is sensitive. In some organizations the document could lead to bad feelings and anger. Stakeholders who believe they are supporting the project, for example, might be frustrated to learn they have been identified by the project team as resisters. The project manager and the project team should be careful to protect the confidentiality of the document.

It is important, however, for the project team to work with stakeholders who are not in the desired category and honestly share with them the team's desires to earn their support or motivate them to take a leadership role. The stakeholder engagement assessment matrix is a dynamic document that will change over time. By taking the appropriate actions, the team can shift the current state of their stakeholders to the right on the matrix and enhance the probability of project success.

Stakeholder Management Plan

The stakeholder management plan is more detailed than the stakeholder engagement assessment matrix. Stakeholder management plans can be formatted many different ways and may include a variety of different pieces of information as necessary. For many organizations, the stakeholder management plan can include everything that is in the stakeholder register (a detailed stakeholder log discussed in Chapter 3), everything that is in the stakeholder's engagement assessment matrix, and a variety of other information.

Potential Information in the Stakeholder Management Plan

The following is a list of the potential information in the stakeholder management plan:

- Consolidated information about communication strategies by group, issue, or other categorization.
    See Section Two, Stakeholder Groups, for more details.
- Best channel for communicating with each stakeholder (for example, e-mail, phone, in person).
    See Chapter 7, Stakeholder Communication, for more detail on stakeholder communication channels.
- Communication channels that will be used to engage groups of stakeholders (for example, in-person meetings, conference calls, virtual meetings).
    See Chapter 7, Stakeholder Communication, for more detail.
- Identification of any topics that must be negotiated.
    See Chapter 12, Negotiation, for more detail.
- Notes on which leadership style will be used for each stakeholder.
    See Chapter 10, Leadership, for detail on leadership styles.
- Notes on what information was shared with each stakeholder on which dates.
- Hot spots that the stakeholders are particularly excited about or concerned about.
- Notes on any constraints the stakeholders may experience during the project (for example, vacations, business trips, standing meetings, other major projects that are demanding their time).

- Tips on how to integrate the stakeholder management plan into other project documents and processes.
- Organizational chart showing the reporting relationships between stakeholders.
- List of which project phases each stakeholder should be included in (initiating, planning, execution, monitoring and controlling, and closing for projects using a waterfall approach; different phases may be used for other approaches).
- List of what will be communicated during each phase.

The project manager should use awareness of project stakeholders and awareness of the project environment to structure the optimal template for the stakeholder management plan. Also, the savvy project manager will recognize that the template is likely to change for each project to make the plan relevant to the project details and environment. As always, project managers should use their expert judgment to determine the details of the stakeholder management plan.

Summary

In this chapter we discussed several categories the project manager can use to analyze stakeholders: power, impact, influence, and interest. These terms are defined in the *PMBOK®* *Guide*, 5th ed. and provide a common language project managers can use to discuss stakeholders. Common project management language is important as individuals and organizations seek to create common terms to explain concepts. Common language is also a goal of organizations seeking to improve their level of project management maturity.

We discussed a tool used to categorize stakeholders, the stakeholder's engagement assessment matrix. The stakeholder's engagement assessment matrix is a simple form that shows the current attitude of each stakeholder and the desired attitude of each stakeholder across five different categories: unsure, resistant, neutral, supportive, and leading. We will use this tool as an input into other project management documents, including the stakeholder register.

In addition, we discussed the stakeholder management plan. The stakeholder management plan is a common document that pulls together different aspects of project stakeholder management. Project managers should customize the stakeholder management plan to their organization and to their specific project.

In the next chapter, Prioritizing Stakeholders, we will introduce the stakeholder register. The stakeholder register is a single document used to capture all the information from the stakeholder engagement assessment matrix and combine it with many other key pieces of data. This single form creates the information backbone required to successfully manage project stakeholders.

Chapter Three

Prioritizing Stakeholders

The key is not to prioritize what's on your schedule, but to schedule your priorities.

Stephen Covey

I n the prior chapter we discussed specific attributes for categorizing project stakeholders. Four of the attributes discussed are:

1. Power—the stakeholder's level of authority.
2. Impact—the stakeholder's ability to affect changes to the project's planning or execution.
3. Interest—the stakeholder's level of concern regarding the project outcomes.
4. Influence—the stakeholder's level of active involvement in the project.

In this chapter, we discuss how to use these attributes, and others, to prioritize project stakeholders. Prioritizing project stakeholders is an important tool for the project manager. Project managers have limited time, and project teams have limited resources to deploy against project stakeholder management. In order to work within these constraints, project managers must determine effective solutions to strategically deploy their time and skills, and the team's time and skills, to work with project stakeholders.

Power and Interest

Without a prioritization plan the stakeholders who complain the most are likely to get the most attention. This is not a strategic way to allocate time. The project manager should not allow the stakeholders to dictate how much time is spent with them. Instead, the project manager must make crisp decisions on how much time to invest in each stakeholder.

With a prioritization plan project managers will understand how to deploy their time. Let's go back to two of the attributes discussed in the prior chapter, power and interest. If we take power and interest and put them into a simple two-by-two matrix, it might look something like the representation in Figure 3.1.

We'll discuss this chart starting with the top right quadrant. This quadrant shows the stakeholders who have a high degree of power and a high level of interest. In other words, stakeholders in this quadrant have a high level of authority and also a high level of concern about the project outcomes. As depicted in this two-by-two matrix, the project manager should manage these stakeholders very closely.

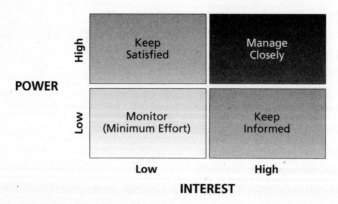

Figure 3.1 Power and Interest Matrix
Source: Adapted from *PMBOK® Guide*, 5th ed.

Next, let's move to the bottom right quadrant. Project stakeholders in this quadrant have a high level of interest but they also have less power. The project manager should keep these stakeholders informed because of their high level of interest in the project. The project manager, however, does not need to manage these project stakeholders as closely as those in the top right quadrant because they do not have as much power. Because project stakeholders in this quadrant have less authority, the strategic project manager understands that less time can be deployed with them.

Next, we look at the top left quadrant. In this quadrant we find project stakeholders with a high amount of power and a low level of interest. Said differently, these project stakeholders have a high level of authority; however, they are not as concerned about project outcomes. The project manager must handle the stakeholders in the top left quadrant carefully because they could easily shift over to the top right quadrant. All the stakeholders in this quadrant would need to do to shift from the top left quadrant to the top right quadrant is to decide that they *wanted* to be more involved. Therefore, the project manager should keep these stakeholders satisfied.

Finally, let's look at the bottom left quadrant. Here we find the project stakeholders with low power and low interest. Project managers, as we discussed, must strategically deploy their time. If there's one quadrant in this chart that the project manager can invest the least amount of time on, it is this one. Stakeholders in the bottom left quadrant do not have much power to change the project outcomes and also don't have much concern about the project, so the project manager should deploy minimal effort with this group of project stakeholders.

It is important to note that the project manager is still monitoring the stakeholders in the bottom left corner. The project manager is not deploying zero effort with these stakeholders. It is possible that some of these project stakeholders will gain more power as the project advances. It is also possible that some of these project stakeholders will become more interested as the project advances. Therefore, the savvy project manager will monitor this group and provide basic communication to them. Very rarely will the project manager encounter a group of project stakeholders who require no effort. Typically, the lowest level of commitment will be to monitor a group of stakeholders.

Panama Canal

The Panama Canal Authority is leading a major project to expand the number of locks. In this project, three new chambers will be added to the two chambers already in operation. This megaproject is also planned to widen and deepen the current navigational channels. Using the 2×2 matrix, let's consider several stakeholders in this project.

Panamanian Government

The Panama Canal is a major economic engine for the country of Panama. Successful completion of the expansion project is very important to the government. Using the chart, the government is powerful and very interested in the outcome. The government is in the top right quadrant. The project managers should closely manage the government.

Unemployed Panamanians

The proposal to expand the canal estimated that 35,000 to 40,000 new jobs would be created by the construction. After completion, it is estimated the canal expansion will yield hundreds of thousands of jobs in its direct and indirect impact to the economy. Unemployed Panamanians are not likely to have as much power as the government. However, they are likely to have a high level of interest in the project's outcome. This stakeholder group is in the bottom right quadrant of the matrix. The project team should keep these stakeholders informed about progress.

Celebrities

A variety of celebrities voiced support for the project. These celebrities are not likely to be as interested in the project as the Panamanian government or unemployed Panamanians. Therefore, celebrities are on the left side of the matrix. Depending on how much power the celebrities have to sway public opinion the project manager will need to either keep them satisfied with current project progress (for celebrities with a lot of power) or monitor them (for celebrities with low power).

SOURCE: "Proposal for the Expansion of the Panama Canal Third Set of Locks Program," Panama Canal Authority, April 24, 2006.

Power and Influence

Next, let's shift our attention to power and influence. Influence measures the active involvement of the project stakeholder. In other words, if stakeholders are very involved in the project, they will have high influence. A project stakeholder who has minimal involvement will have low influence. For some, the words *power* and *influence* may sound very similar. However, as written in the *PMBOK® Guide*, power refers to the stakeholder's level of authority, whereas influence, as stated in Chapter Two, refers to the stakeholder's level of involvement. (See Figure 3.2.)

Involvement is another way to think about influence. In today's hurried environment, many project stakeholders find themselves on numerous teams. In addition to their involvement on the teams, they may also have day-to-day management or operational responsibilities.

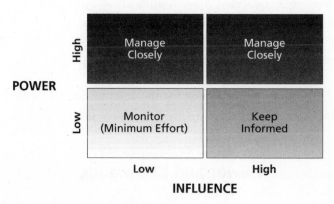

Figure 3.2 Power and Influence Matrix
Source: Adapted from *PMBOK® Guide*, 5th ed.

The project manager can get a different perspective on this chart by replacing the word *influence* with the word *involvement*.

Figure 3.2 shows a power/influence grid. It is populated the same way as the power/impact grid with one exception—the top left corner. The top left quadrant shows stakeholders with a high degree of power and a low amount of influence. Unlike the power/impact grid that showed the stakeholders' level of interest, in this case the stakeholders in the top left may be very interested but simply unable to attend meetings. These stakeholders should be managed as closely as those in the top right quadrant. Project stakeholders in the top left quadrant may make themselves available for key decision meetings at later points in the project. The project manager will want to keep them informed and make sure they are aware and supportive of the project.

This will be challenging for the project manager. As evidenced by these stakeholders' lack of involvement in the team they may be difficult to track down for meetings and phone calls. The project manager will need to be creative in how he or she communicates with project stakeholders in the top left corner. Virtual technologies, such as virtual meetings and video phone calls, may be deployed to keep stakeholders in the top left quadrant informed.

See Chapter 8, Managing Stakeholders in a Virtual World, for more details on working with stakeholders who are remotely located or who travel extensively.

Project stakeholders in the other three cells in this matrix are managed in a similar manner as the power/impact matrix. Stakeholders in the top right quadrant have significant power and are actively involved. The project manager should manage these stakeholders closely. Stakeholders in the bottom right quadrant do not have as much power in the organization but are active in the project. These stakeholders should be kept informed. Stakeholders in the bottom left quadrant are the best candidates for the least amount of effort. These stakeholders are not actively involved and have limited power.

Power and Knowledge

Knowledge is the measure of each stakeholder's level of project-specific knowledge. The project manager is best served by stakeholders with

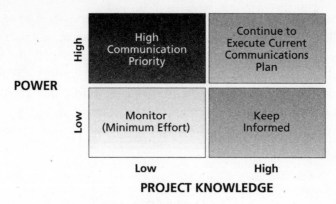

Figure 3.3 Power and Knowledge Matrix
Source: © 2012 Roeder Consulting.

deep knowledge of the project. Knowledgeable stakeholders are better able to contribute valuable thoughts and ideas to the project team. Also, knowledgeable project team stakeholders are better able to execute against the plan because they know what the plan is and how to get there.

If we map power against project knowledge it might look something like the representation in Figure 3.3.

Let's begin with the top right corner. In the top right corner we find project stakeholders with high power and a high level of knowledge about the project. Our current communications plan is working for these stakeholders as evidenced by their high level of project knowledge. These stakeholders get it. The project manager should continue to execute the current plan.

Next, let's look at the top left quadrant. The top left quadrant represents stakeholders with a high degree of power but with limited knowledge about the project. The project manager must work to increase the level of knowledge of these stakeholders. These stakeholders may show up at meetings later in the process and cause disruptions if they are not fully knowledgeable on the project. Communicating project information to this group of stakeholders should be a top priority.

In the bottom right corner we see stakeholders with low power but high knowledge. Since these project stakeholders have less power to influence the project, they represent a lower communication priority than the project stakeholders on the top row. The project manager should continue to keep these stakeholders informed about project status.

Finally, in the bottom left quadrant we find project stakeholders with low power and low project knowledge. This group requires the least attention of any of the groups in this chart. These project stakeholders should be monitored and given minimal effort in regard to communications.

Custom Matrices

Additional insights can be learned about project stakeholders by combining any of the attributes just discussed. For example, an interest/knowledge grid will show the project manager how involved the most knowledgeable stakeholders are. In addition, the project manager and the project team should consider creating their own attributes that are specific to their project and creating custom matrices with these attributes.

In projects where the time line is absolutely critical the project team might categorize and prioritize stakeholders according to their track record of delivering tasks on time. Stakeholders with critical tasks and a poor timeliness rating may be the top priority for the project manager's attention. Project teams should experiment with the categories and prioritization schemes to find those that are most relevant for their particular project.

Stakeholder Register

The project stakeholder register is the central document for tracking project stakeholders. In this section we discuss the different fields in the stakeholder register, how to complete them, and the role this document plays in increasing the probability of project success. Also, we discuss how the project stakeholder register relates to other technical project management documents.

Stakeholder Register as a Tool

The project stakeholder register is the primary tool used for organizing information related to each project stakeholder. The stakeholder register has five sections:

1. *Contact information.* In this section the basic contact information for each stakeholder is provided. Information includes the stakeholder's name, title, location, and how to contact the stakeholder.
2. *Category.* This section characterizes each stakeholder across the attributes of power, interest, influence, and impact. Based on responses to these inputs, the project manager will rank the priority of each stakeholder.
3. *Project role.* The project role section identifies which group(s) the stakeholder is part of, which phase or phases he or she is most interested in, and the higher-level tasks assigned to the stakeholder.
4. *Status.* In the status section the project manager shows the stakeholder's level of support.
5. *Priority.* This section contains the prioritization rating for how much time and effort the project manager should invest in the stakeholder.

Comprehensive, Holistic Stakeholder Register

It is important to note that this stakeholder register is more detailed and holistic than the one depicted in the *PMBOK*® *Guide*. The project manager will benefit from having a single document that can be used to track and manage stakeholders. The single document, the stakeholder register, should include contact information and content information that represents the stakeholder's categorization, group affiliations, attitudes, and so on. In this book, therefore, we present a detailed and holistic stakeholder register that pulls various stakeholder information into a single easy-to-use document.

Context of the Stakeholder Register

As the primary tool used to track and manage project stakeholders, the stakeholder register is in the middle of various project document inputs and outputs. The stakeholder register inputs include information from the categorization of stakeholders, the status of stakeholders, and the stakeholder engagement assessment matrix. We will discuss each of these in more detail.

Inputs into the Stakeholder Register

The stakeholder register is a consolidated report that collects information from other documents and decisions. Stakeholders are easier to track and manage if key information about them is in a single document.

Categorization Inputs

In Chapter 2, Categorizing Stakeholders, we discussed different stakeholder categories—power, interest, influence, and impact. Each stakeholder's rating across these categories is an input into the stakeholder register.

For more detail on each of these categories, see Chapter 2, Categorizing Stakeholders.

Stakeholder Status Inputs

In Chapter 11, Buy-In, we will discuss how to analyze stakeholders' attitudes about our project. A stakeholder's status can be unsure, resistant, neutral, supportive, or leading. This information is an input into the status column of the stakeholder register.

For more detail on status, see Chapter 11, Buy-In.

Stakeholder Engagement Assessment Matrix Inputs

In Chapter 2, Categorizing Stakeholders, we discussed the stakeholder engagement assessment matrix. In this matrix the project manager identifies the current status of each stakeholder (his or her level of support), and the desired status. The status column in the stakeholder register consolidates all of the information from the stakeholder engagement assessment matrix into a single column. Using a lettering convention discussed in the following pages, the project manager can streamline all of the information in the stakeholder engagement assessment matrix into a two-digit code.

For more detail on the stakeholder engagement assessment matrix, see Chapter 2, Categorizing Stakeholders.

Stakeholder Register Detailed Instructions

In this section we discuss how to populate each column in the stakeholder register. See Figure 3.4 for a representation of a stakeholder register.

Contact Information

The contact information on the register consists of the following:

- *Stakeholder name.* Enter the stakeholder's first and last name, as well as any nicknames or preferred names as required.
- *Title.* Enter the stakeholder's formal title in the organization.
- *Location.* Enter the primary geographic location of the stakeholder. If the stakeholder travels frequently or has multiple office locations, list the location considered the stakeholder's home base.
- *Business address.* Enter the stakeholder's professional mailing address.
- *Phone number.* Enter the stakeholder's preferred telephone number, and indicate if it is a mobile phone (M), office phone (O), or personal line (P). If available, also enter secondary phone numbers.
- *E-mail address.* Enter the stakeholder's preferred e-mail address.

The category section on the register includes the following:

- *Power.* Power is a measure of the stakeholder's level of authority within the project. Indicate how much power the stakeholder has by using a rating of high (H), medium (M), or low (L).
- *Interest.* Interest is a measure of the stakeholder's level of concern with regard to the project. Indicate how much interest the stakeholder has in the project by using a rating of high (H), medium (M), or low (L).
- *Influence.* Influence is a measure of how actively involved the stakeholder is in the project. Indicate the stakeholder's level of

Stakeholder Name	Contact Information						Category							Project Role		Status
	Title	Location	Business Address	Phone # (primary)	Phone # (secondary)	E-Mail Address	Power	Interest	Influence	Impact	Knowledge	Priority	Group	Project Phase with Interest	Project Tasks	Support Neutral/ Resist
1																
2																
3																
4																
5																
6																
7																
8																
9																
10																
11																
12																

Figure 3.4 Stakeholder Register

influence over the project by using a rating of high (H), medium (M), or low (L).

- *Impact.* Impact is a measure of the stakeholder's ability to effect changes to the project. Indicate the stakeholder's level of influence by using a rating of high (H), medium (M), or low (L).
- *Knowledge.* Knowledge is a measure of the stakeholder's level of knowledge of the project details. Indicate the stakeholder's level of knowledge by using a rating of high (H), medium (M), or low (L).

The priority column on the register includes the following:

- Based on the information in the preceding five columns, the project team should assign a priority to each project stakeholder as follows:
  - Priority one (1)—the most critical project stakeholders. Top-priority stakeholders have a high ranking in three or more categories.
  - Priority two (2)—important stakeholders. Important stakeholders have a high ranking in two or more categories.
  - Priority three (3)—stakeholders to keep engaged in the process. Priority three stakeholders have a high ranking in one category.
  - Priority four (4)—stakeholders who should be monitored. Stakeholders without a high ranking in any category are priority four.

Prioritization Scale

The prioritization scale provided here is a benchmark. Based on project circumstances, the project manager may choose to score priorities differently. For example, a stakeholder with two high ratings and three medium ratings may be considered priority one because the areas where the stakeholder received the high rankings are of particular importance to the project. The project manager and the project team should use their judgment when assigning priorities.

There may be gray areas where the categories don't exactly reflect the level of importance the project team wants to assign to each stakeholder. In these cases it is advisable to put a note on the stakeholder register indicating the reasons for the individual stakeholder's priority level.

The project role on the register includes the following:

- *Stakeholder group.* Using Section Two of this book as a reference, enter which group(s) the stakeholder is part of. Possible group options are project team, executive, external, and stakeholder subject to the change. Note that phantom stakeholders are not included because, by definition, they have not been identified. When they are identified, they should be placed into the appropriate group. A stakeholder may be a member of one or more groups. For example, an executive member of the project team would be a member of both the executive stakeholder group and the project team group.

  See Section Two, Stakeholder Groups, for more detail on how to assign stakeholders to groups.
- *Project phase with interest.* Information can be entered into this column using one of three formats.
  - *Option one.* Categorize stakeholders according to which of the five traditional waterfall project phases are of interest to them. These project phases are initiating (I), planning (P), executing (E), monitoring and controlling (M), and closing (C). Stakeholders may be in one phase, multiple phases, or all of these project phases.
  - *Option two.* Categorize stakeholders according to some other project management process or framework such as agile.
  - *Option three.* Categorize stakeholders according to the delineations indicated in the work breakdown structure. The work breakdown structure is a decomposition of all project tasks into their smallest parts. The project phase column can be used to indicate which aspects of the project work breakdown structure are applicable to each stakeholder. Project stakeholders may be most interested in only one category of the work breakdown structure, multiple categories of the work breakdown structure, or in some cases all aspects of the work breakdown structure.
- *Project tasks.* List the higher-level tasks the stakeholder is responsible for. The project manager is encouraged to list the two or three primary tasks each stakeholder is working on. In order to keep this document at a high level and easily usable, project tasks should be brief.

The status on the register includes the following:

- In the status column, list the stakeholder's level of support for the project. Using the following lettering convention, the project manager can streamline all of the information from the stakeholder engagement assessment matrix into a single column. As an added benefit, the two-digit codes entered into the status column will have no meaning to an uninformed individual looking at the stakeholder register. This is a useful way to protect the confidential information on each stakeholder's level of support.

    Identifier from stakeholder engagement assessment matrix:
    C = Current
    D = Desired
    Level of support:
    U = Unsure
    R = Resistant
    N = Neutral
    S = Supportive
    L = Leading
    Examples of combining these two codes:
    CU = Currently unsure
    CN = Currently neutral
    DL = Desired to be leading
    DS = Desired to be supportive

The two different letter codes can be combined in many different combinations. In most cases the desired state will be either "S" for supportive or "L" for leading. In some cases, however, the desired status may be "N" for neutral.

The stakeholder register should be completed with an appropriate level of detail. Each project team will determine what is appropriate for their project. Some project teams will expand the size of the cells and use the register to track a higher level of detail. Other teams will get the best use out of the register by entering only high-level information. In general, the register is intended to be a snapshot and not a detailed planning document. The project manager and the project team,

---

From Resistant to Neutral

In a perfect situation all stakeholders are leaders. Realistically, however, there are likely to be some stakeholders who do not support the project. For some of these individuals, the project manager may strive to turn their resistance into support. For other stakeholders, the most reasonable goal may be to shift them from a resistant to a neutral position. A neutral stakeholder will not actively work against the project. If the project manager enjoys stakeholders who are either supportive or neutral, the project is likely to succeed.

---

however, should deploy their expert judgment to ensure the register fits their needs. The project manager should update the stakeholder register regularly, adding stakeholders, removing stakeholders, and making other adjustments as necessary.

Outputs from the Stakeholder Register

The stakeholder register creates information that is used as an input into other documents in the project management process. In this book we have added to the amount of information included in the stakeholder register. Therefore, some of this information will not have a direct input into other project management forms as outlined in the *PMBOK*® *Guide*. However, core components of the stakeholder register, such as contact information and group affiliations, are direct inputs into other project management documents.

The project team may choose to customize the documents that are downstream from the stakeholder register to incorporate the expanded information in the register into their formal project management framework. This is encouraged and will lead to an increased probability of project success. The two key documents that are downstream from the stakeholder register are the stakeholder management plan and the communications management plan.

Stakeholder Management Plan

The stakeholder management plan is a detailed document depicting many different aspects of project stakeholder management. The project manager should create a customized stakeholder management plan based on the situation, the unique stakeholders, and the project objectives. There are numerous variations on the stakeholder management plan.

See Chapter 2, Categorizing Stakeholders, for more detail on the stakeholder management plan.

Communications Management Plan

The project communications management plan is a central document that shows what is communicated to whom, and when it should be communicated. The stakeholder register includes information that will flow into the project communications management plan.

Common stakeholder register inputs into the project communications management plan include:

- *Contact information.* Addresses, phone numbers, e-mail addresses, and location information will all be useful inputs into the project communications management plan. In some cases, this information may already be in the project management communications plan and can be used to populate the stakeholder register.
- *Priority.* The priority column in the stakeholder register ranks all project stakeholders on a scale from 1 to 4, with 1 being the highest priority and 4 being lowest priority. The ranking will impact the project communications for each stakeholder. For example, a stakeholder with a higher ranking is likely to receive more frequent communication and more detailed communication.
- *Project role.* Each of the project role columns in the stakeholder register has an influence on the communications management plan. The project team may have a communications plan for each group, for each project phase, and for each critical project task. These columns in the stakeholder register indicate which stakeholders should receive each communication.
- *Status.* Communications strategies are heavily influenced by the code entered into the status column in the stakeholder register.

The communications strategy, for example, for a stakeholder who is currently supportive will be different from the communications strategy for a stakeholder who is currently resistant and is desired to be neutral.

See Chapter 11, Buy-In, for more information on techniques to shift a stakeholder's status into one more desirable for the team.

Project Management Plan

The project management plan, in a traditional waterfall approach, is the central document to monitor and control all aspects of the project. The stakeholder management plan and the communication management plan just described are inputs into the project management plan. Project management plans vary by organization and by project. The project manager and the project team should ensure integration between the stakeholder register and the project management plan.

Summary

In summary, project managers must strategically deploy their time and energy when working with stakeholders. Time may be the project manager's scarcest resource. Time must be used wisely when managing stakeholders. In this chapter we developed a tangible set of frameworks the project manager should use to determine how much time to allocate to each stakeholder. We also discussed several two-by-two matrices the project manager can use to evaluate and prioritize stakeholders. Project managers and project teams are encouraged to develop customized matrices for their specific projects.

Also, we looked at the stakeholder register, the primary document the project manager uses to track and manage stakeholders. We presented a comprehensive and holistic stakeholder register that is more detailed than the one offered in the *PMBOK® Guide*. The stakeholder register is integrated into the project management technical skills process. We discussed other project management documents that are inputs into the stakeholder register, as well as several documents downstream from the stakeholder register, such as the project management plan.

It is important for the project manager to complete the technical project management forms discussed in this book. Project stakeholder documents should be updated on an ongoing basis. Stakeholders and situations change frequently in the project environment. These forms, however, do not manage the project. The project manager must manage the project. Savvy project managers will invest more of their time interacting with stakeholders, communicating with the team, and so on, and less of their time filling out forms. The forms are an aid.

The project manager must work with different groups of stakeholders: project team members, executives, external stakeholders, stakeholders subject to the change, and a group we call phantom stakeholders. The project manager can simplify the process of project stakeholder management by understanding each of these groups and tailoring his or her approach accordingly. In Section Two of this book we focus on project stakeholder groups.

Section Two

STAKEHOLDER GROUPS

Section Two discusses five stakeholder groups: project team stakeholders, executive stakeholders, external stakeholders, stakeholders subject to the change, and phantom stakeholders. Stakeholders in each group may have much in common with one another. Section Two is divided into three chapters: Project Team Members, Executive Stakeholders, and Other Stakeholders.

Chapter 4, Project Team Members, discusses techniques to manage the project team. Project managers are likely to spend most of their time working with project team stakeholders. Chapter 4 discusses how to build relationships with the project team and create an environment that is poised for success.

Chapter 5, Executive Stakeholders, focuses on working collaboratively with the executives directing the project. In many cases the executive stakeholders are the single most powerful stakeholder group. In this chapter the project manager learns techniques to harness the power of executive stakeholders to the benefit of the project team.

Chapter 6, Other Stakeholders, explains three additional stakeholder groups: external stakeholders, stakeholders subject to the change, and phantom stakeholders. In this chapter the project manager gains techniques to work with each of these groups to increase the probability of project success.

Chapter Four

Project Team Members

Coming together is a beginning, staying together is progress,
and working together is success.

Henry Ford

P roject team members assist the project manager in delivering
project success. They often invest considerable time in the project's
design and execution and feel a strong sense of ownership over the
project. The savvy project manager nourishes this feeling of ownership
among team members and keeps the project team actively engaged.
Project managers may spend more time with project team stakeholders
than with any other stakeholder group. In this chapter we discuss how to
deliver successful project outcomes with project team members.

Who They Are

Project team members are the individuals most actively involved in
delivering the project. They typically work closely with the project
manager to deliver project results. Project team members may be
involved in each of the five phases of the project lifecycle:

1. *Initiating.* Team members may assist in drafting the charter and other initiation documents.
2. *Planning.* Team members can help estimate the project time line, budget, key milestones, and so on.
3. *Executing.* Project team members help manage stakeholders, initiate change requests, and provide overall support for project execution.
4. *Monitoring and controlling.* Team members may be involved in the approval process for project change requests. Also, team members may track and control various project metrics such as earned value.
5. *Closing.* Team members may help capture lessons learned, close out vendor contracts, and assist with team celebrations.

This list shows just a few of the activities that may involve project team members. In some organizations team members may be recruited onto projects after the initiation phase is already complete. Indeed, the project manager himself or herself may not begin work on a project until the initiation phase is complete. When team members begin working on the project, it is the project manager's responsibility to quickly educate team members about the project and provide specific direction on how each team member can contribute.

Team members may roll off the project at any point. Frequently, project team members complete their work before the closing phase. It is common for a slimmed-down version of the project team to be responsible for closing out projects, thereby freeing up the other resources to move on to the next project or responsibility.

Project teams are structured in many different ways. Project team members may be:

- Full-time, part-time, or involved on an ad hoc basis.
- Dedicated to the project or borrowed from their regular jobs.
- Employed by the same organization as the project manager or by a different organization.
- Subject matter experts or generalists.
- Project customers and/or sponsors.

The project team includes the project manager, people who are actively involved with managing the project, and others in support functions. Time commitment to the project is likely to vary by team member.

Tips for Managing Project Team Stakeholders

The successful project manager must be an effective team leader. In this section we discuss tips on how to effectively launch project teams and engage members on an ongoing basis. Most project managers do not have project stakeholders reporting directly to them,[1] so they must become skilled at keeping the project team motivated, engaged, and actively working on the project through means other than direct supervision. This requires a special set of skills.

See Chapter 10, Leadership, for additional insight into project leadership and further detail on the percentage of project managers with direct stakeholder reports.

Time Commitment

Project team members are likely to invest more time in the project than any other stakeholders. When identifying stakeholders to serve on project teams, the project manager should pay attention to the amount of time that person will have for contributing to the team. Even the best resource may not be a good fit if the person does not have time to work on the project. If possible, project managers should get dedicated resources for their projects. Dedicated resources focus solely on the project's success without the distractions that arise from other operational or project-based responsibilities.

For larger projects it is advisable to have at least several full-time dedicated resources. It is not unusual for organizations to assign people to project teams without relieving them of other day-to-day responsibilities. This can often lead to serious resource constraints. Even the person with the best intentions may have a difficult time conducting a full-time job and also contributing to a project team. Further, many individuals and organizations today are involved with multiple projects. This compounds the problem.

---

[1]Roeder Consulting webinar survey data, 2010 and 2012.

Project Team Kickoff

A formal kickoff meeting is recommended for all projects. A project kickoff meeting has three primary goals:

1. Break the ice with team members and begin building relationships.
2. Share the project scope, budget, and key deliverables with the team.
3. Communicate to each team member their role in achieving the project deliverables.

Relationships among team members are an important aspect of project success. Project managers may find that project team members are loyal to each other and willing to work diligently to prevent disappointing one of their teammates. The deeper the relationships that project team members have with each other and the deeper the trust, the higher the probability that team members will establish a group bond and a strong desire to achieve success. The project manager should begin facilitating these ties and relationships early in the process with an appropriate kickoff. There are many different types of exercises that can be used to break the ice during a project kickoff.

Breaking the Ice When in Person

Icebreakers are intended to pull the project team together and build relationships. If done correctly, an effective icebreaker will motivate the team while simultaneously helping them learn about each other. Highly effective teams have a sixth sense about what their teammates are thinking and doing. Consider the case of a basketball team that is working together as a unit. They know where others are on the court, even if behind them. They anticipate when a teammate will charge the basket so they can prepare for a quick pass to the teammate. Effective project teams have a similar sixth sense they deploy to understand what other team members are doing and why they are doing it.

Icebreakers, however, can also be a demoralizing experience for team members. If the icebreaker is perceived as a silly or unnecessary exercise, the team members may feel belittled. They may actually emerge from a poor icebreaker *less* interested in following the project manager and helping the team. Effective icebreakers should be authentic, well-planned, and positive.

Attributes of a Successful Icebreaker

- *Authentic.* The individual leading the icebreaker must come across as sincere and genuine in his or her interest in the team's success. People can tell when a facilitator is simply going through the motions and not investing genuine concern and interest into the exercise.
- *Well-planned.* The icebreaker should not be an afterthought that is quickly thrown together just before the meeting starts. The facilitator should think through different scenarios that might occur during the icebreaker and how to manage them. The facilitator should have a basic understanding of the group before the icebreaker begins and tailor the exercise to the group's needs and interests.
- *Positive.* Icebreakers should make people feel good about themselves and good about the team they are joining. The facilitator should model a positive attitude for the team. Also, the icebreaking exercise should bring out the positive side of participants.

"Vote with Your Body" Icebreaker

Begin this exercise by asking everyone on the project team to stand up in the meeting room. Explain to the individuals that they will be asked questions. They are to respond by standing in a certain place in the room. Where they stand will depend on the question and their response. After everyone has answered the question and is in their place, the project manager will call on a few people to discuss their answer. A list of sample questions follows:

- Explain that the room is a map of the world. Point out where the continents are in the room. Ask team members to stand in the country where they were born. Give people time to figure out where their country is and move to that spot on the floor. After everyone is in their place, ask several members of the team to talk about their place of birth. There are many variants of the geographic exercise. If the team is entirely based in the United States, the project manager can explain that the room is a map of the

United States, and might ask people to stand in the state where they were born or where they went to high school or college.

- Divide the room into sections for each functional area in your organization. Appoint accounting, for example, to one corner of the room, operations to another corner, marketing to the center of the room, and so on. Ask each person to stand in the part of the room that is associated with that individual's function. After everyone is in place, ask one or two people to explain why their function is excited about the new project.

- Ask the Project Management Professionals (PMPs®)[2] to stand on one side of the room and those who are not PMPs® to stand on the other side of the room. Ask the PMPs® how long they have had their designation. Ask the most experienced PMP® to tell the story of how he or she initially got into project management. Then, go to the other side of the room and ask if any of those team members plan to earn their PMP®. This exercise can be repeated for different professional credentials, academic degrees, and so on.

- Ask team members how long they have been working on projects. Create a continuum across the room with 20 years or more of experience on one side, one year or less on the other side, and 10 years or so in the middle. Ask the most experienced people what sorts of projects they have worked on and their number-one tip for the rest of the team. Ask people on the other side of the continuum what they are looking forward to in the new project.

Keep people moving around the room. Be creative with the types of questions asked and how people are positioned. This exercise gets people moving, facilitates team relationships, and is fun. Each question from the project manager should not last more than a few minutes. Keep the exercise moving.

---

[2]PMP® is a registered mark of the Project Management Institute.

Breaking the Ice in a Virtual Environment

Team-building exercises can be done in virtual teams, too. It is always best to get the team to meet in person; however, this is not always realistic. Budget constraints, travel restrictions, scheduling constraints, and a handful of other issues can lead to challenges planning in-person kickoff meetings.

Using an icebreaker to build team relationships and rapport may be even more important in a virtual environment than in an in-person environment. Extra effort is required to help virtual team members feel like they are a valued part of the team. When in person, the project manager can shake hands, pat people on the back, build relationships over lunch or a coffee, and so on. In an in-person environment there are typically opportunities for casual hallway conversations and informal get-togethers. These sorts of casual get-togethers typically do not happen in a virtual environment. The team meets only during scheduled times and only if there is a specific goal to accomplish. This does not afford an opportunity for the bonding that occurs in more casual interactions. Therefore, the project manager should plan into the initial virtual team meetings structured activities to build relationships.

When in a virtual environment, the project manager should first select a virtual tool that is robust. An in-person meeting, as discussed, is the most robust way to launch the team. The next best way is a virtual meeting with live streaming video and audio. There are a variety of technologies commonly available that will enable this functionality. If live video is not an option, the next best option is a conference call or some sort of live audio line. E-mail is the worst way to launch the team.

Learn more about the continuum of robustness for communication channels in Chapter 8, Managing Stakeholders in a Virtual World.

The "vote with your body" exercise described for the in-person icebreakers can be done in a virtual environment with one adjustment. Instead of having people physically move around a room, simulate the room on the screen. Use technology that enables individuals to place pointers or some other mark on the screen. The project manager might say, for example, "If you are an experienced project manager, click your symbol or type your name on the right-hand side of the screen. If you are on your first project, then place your symbol or type your name all the way on the left-hand side of the screen."

When working in a virtual environment with audio but without live visual technology as just described, the facilitator can select a different icebreaker based on verbal feedback. The facilitator might ask people to name the country where they were born, or the number of years they've been managing projects. An effective facilitator will use the team's responses as an opening into a lively conversation. When designing the icebreaker, be sure to follow the principles outlined earlier in this chapter. Effective icebreakers are authentic, well-planned, and positive.

Group Directory

A group directory, including contact information and photographs, is an effective way to build team relationships and communication. The project manager, or his or her designee, can create this directory early in the project. In today's virtual environment it is not unusual for people to work together on project teams yet never meet in person. Photographs and a brief description of team members can go a long way in building relationships. Relationships are further enhanced by adding into the directory team members' hobbies, educational backgrounds, favorite vacation spots, moments of fame they'd like to share, or any other information that will establish common ground and interest among team members.

Keeping the Team Engaged

It is important to keep all project stakeholders engaged, excited, and aware of the project. Active engagement becomes even more crucial with project team stakeholders. A motivated team is more likely to be a successful team. This starts from the very beginning. The project manager should thoughtfully and personally invite people to be on the team. A personal note or phone call welcoming the individual to the team is a great start.

Initial contact might include basic details on the scope of the project, a list of other members of the team, why the team member is uniquely qualified to serve on the team, and personal thoughts from the project manager on why he or she is enthusiastic about the new project. This initial contact, when done correctly, will provide the new team members with a positive feeling about themselves, the team, and the project manager. A confident project manager will improve the team members' confidence that the project will be successful. Everyone wants to be part of a successful team.

Be Confident

A confident project manager is more likely to be a successful project manager. Project team members can sense the project manager's level of confidence. Team members are likely to be more motivated if they sense a project manager who is strong, in control, and knowledgeable.

Project environments often have a lot of uncertainty. This uncertainty can lead the less confident project manager to be skittish, unsure, and tepid. Project team members will sense this trepidation. Team members are less likely to follow a project manager with these characteristics.

It is important, however, not to be overconfident. There is a line between confident and cocky. Cocky project managers are overly impressed with their knowledge and abilities. This is a turn-off for team members. Cocky project managers are also less likely to notice the reality around them. Cockiness can close in individuals and lead them to rely on only their insular perception of reality. They will miss cues around them that may be screaming out a different reality. Cockiness is not a path to project success.

After the project team has been successfully launched, the project manager's next challenge is to keep the team actively engaged and motivated. There is often excitement and enthusiasm at the beginning of the project, but this excitement and enthusiasm may wane as the project advances. The smart project manager will sense when the team needs an injection of motivation. At this point the project manager should call for a team lunch, a fun team activity, or some other way to bring the team together in an enjoyable environment.

These get-togethers do not need to take a lot of time. Project team members may be very busy and juggling competing constraints on their time. There may not be interest in a lengthy team activity. Another approach, in this situation, is to schedule a working team meeting that doubles as a motivational exercise for the team. Using this combined approach, actual project work is being done so team members who are reluctant to give up their time for a team social event are more likely to attend.

Having Fun While Getting Work Done

A project manager is leading a team through a particularly challenging exercise to create a work breakdown structure (WBS). The WBS decomposes all of the project work into digestible pieces and enables a clear understanding of who is responsible for each piece.

The project team is on a deadline and must have the WBS completed by the end of the month. The project manager also realizes that the team is getting worn down and morale is suffering. Consequently, the project manager decides to call together a motivational session that will also serve as a WBS working session. The goal of the session will be twofold: (1) complete the WBS and (2) provide a fun environment to recharge the team.

In the following days the project team reserves a private conference room in the corporate offices that has windows, sunlight, plenty of space to mingle, and lots of wall space to post drawings of the WBS. The project manager arranges for food to be brought into the meeting, and asks for a volunteer to bring a set of speakers and some music. Other thinking devices are solicited as well, such as stress balls and brain twisters.

The result is a fun and productive meeting. The team enjoys food, music, and lively discussion. They also spend time at the walls where the draft WBS is posted. They complete the WBS. The team has completed their deliverable and also rekindled their enthusiasm for the project.

Celebrating Success

When projects are completed successfully, the project manager should celebrate with the project team. Regrettably, it is all too common for organizations and project team members to move from one project to the next without any sort of closure, acknowledgment, or team celebration. In-person celebrations might include:

- Team dinner.
- Awards ceremony.
- Public recognition at an organizational meeting.
- Executive recognition event.
- Fun closing team meeting with each person sharing a favorite story of a notable moment in the project.

Parties are possible virtually also. The project manager can pull everyone into a live online session and conduct an awards ceremony or some other form of celebration. Creative teams find ways to coordinate individual in-person celebrations into the virtual team celebration. For example, individuals at different locations might purchase a cake or some kind of treat and then cut the cake or share the treat virtually at the same time in the virtual meeting. Other ideas for virtual celebrations are:

- Blog or wiki with team stories.
- Ship gifts or awards to team members.
- E-mail gift certificates.
- Virtual closing team meeting with storytelling and photographs.
- A shared site with team photos and other fun material.

The Extended Project Management Team

Projects are often cross-functional and require work from stakeholders in various groups or functional areas. Individuals performing work should be considered project team members. If the group of individuals grows to be a large number, more than 10 or 12 people, the project manager should consider creating a core project team and an extended project team.

A Tale of Two Hats

Try this technique as a way to encourage project team members to get their work completed on time and also to recognize exemplary contributions.

The project manager brings two hats to every team meeting. One hat is the "I'm behind schedule" hat, and the second is the "I figured out a brilliant solution" hat.

Any time someone in the project team falls behind on a milestone, the person must wear the "I'm behind schedule" hat for the entire meeting. Project team stakeholders will try to avoid wearing this hat. This is an effective way to encourage people to be on time with their deliverables.

Any time during the meeting, or during the project, that a team member develops a new and effective solution to one of the team's problems, then the person gets the opportunity to wear the "I figured out a brilliant solution" hat. Everyone wants to have this hat on.

As an added motivator, the project manager might take pictures of people in their hats and post them where the team can see them. In a virtual environment, the project manager might use photographs of team members and virtually add the hats to their heads. The project manager will want to be careful not to offend anyone and will have to strike the right tone to make this exercise effective but also fun.

The core project team represents the stakeholders who are heavily involved in the project. The core project team meets on a regular basis to share updates, plan contingencies, and monitor and control project performance. The core team monitors progress against scope, budget, quality, and so on.

The extended project team meets less frequently or, in some cases, not at all as a group. The extended team includes stakeholders who may have responsibility for one task or one phase of the project. The project manager should engage extended project team stakeholders and keep them on track. However, these extended project team members do not require the same level of involvement in the project as the core team members.

Creation of a core project team and an extended project team will help the project manager control all project team stakeholders without creating a day-to-day core team that is too large. A team that is too large is difficult to manage and control.

Watch-Outs

Project teams can be a powerful alliance of individuals working together to earn project success. If not managed properly, however, a project team can become a disorganized, unmotivated, and confused group of skeptics. The most common pitfalls that lead to ineffective teams are described next.

Lack of Motivation

Motivated project team members are more effective contributors. The project manager may sense that certain project team members are not contributing to their full abilities because they have not committed themselves to the project.

The project manager may be able to motivate a team member through chatting over a coffee or on the telephone. Sometimes, caring and personal contact from the project leader is enough of a boost to give project team members the motivation they need. In other cases, there may be more serious issues underlying the team member's motivation, such as personal problems or professional challenges. The project manager should use awareness to uncover the source of the poor motivation, then react accordingly, understanding that some motivational issues might be beyond the project manager's control.

Poor Direction

Most project team members genuinely want to do a good job. Frustration occurs when they do not know *how* to do a good job. They may have been given an assignment they do not know how to complete.

Instead of asking the project manager for help, which the project team members may incorrectly consider a display of weakness or ignorance, they may continue to struggle with the problem on their own, never achieving the full value they can offer the project team.

The savvy project manager recognizes when a conscientious stakeholder is struggling. The project manager should diplomatically offer to help without making the stakeholder feel like he or she has failed. After the lines of communication are open, the project manager and team member can work together to get the tasks back on plan.

Project managers can proactively minimize the number of confused stakeholders by providing crisp and specific directions early in the project. They must adapt their style, however, to different team members. Less experienced team members may require very specific direction, whereas more experienced team members are likely to benefit more from higher-level, more goal-focused guidance.

For more detail on tailoring leadership styles to individual stakeholders, see Chapter 10, Leadership.

Overburdened Team Members

Many people are working harder than ever before. As organizations streamline operations, the remaining staff ends up with more work to do. Many report being overburdened with multiple projects in addition to their regular day-to-day responsibilities. Overburdened project team members, despite their best intentions, simply may not have enough time to do the work required of them from the project team.

The effective project manager will quickly recognize the overburdened team member and develop a list of potential solutions. Possible solutions might include shifting the work to a different stakeholder, working with the overburdened team member to free up more time for project work, or finding more efficient ways to have the stakeholder complete the project work. Using their awareness, the project manager and the impacted project team member will likely develop other solutions, too. The key is to have open communication with the team member and collaboratively figure out how to achieve project success.

Loyalty to Team above the Project Manager

In some cases the team members may protect each other at the expense of the larger mission. As stated earlier, it is important to build team relationships. The team will be more effective when members bond together and develop a sense that they do not want to let down the group. When this leads to behaviors, however, that shield the team from reality or that keep the facts from being reported to the project manager, it is an indication that the team is dysfunctional. Since the team was put in place to achieve the mission, this is a scenario likely to lead to a failed project. The project manager should take actions to maintain the team's bonds while simultaneously reminding the team that there is a larger goal that must be achieved.

Summary

This chapter, the first chapter in Section Two of this book, was focused on project team stakeholders because project managers are likely to spend most of their time with this group. Also, the project team conducts most of the project work. Therefore, it is critical to keep project team members motivated, informed, and actively engaged with the project.

Effective management of a project team begins with a proper kickoff. Project kickoff meetings must inform team members about the mission before them. Team members are more effective if they understand the higher-level project goals and deliverables and why they are important to their organization. Also, kickoff meetings should begin to build team relationships and commitment. Kickoff meetings can be conducted in-person or virtually.

Effective project managers are confident without being overconfident. Also, successful project managers use their awareness to determine when project team members are not achieving their full potential due to obstacles such as poor motivation, lack of proper direction, or being overburdened with too much work. In many cases, a personal conversation with the impacted project team member will uncover the path to resolution.

In the next chapter we shift our attention to the stakeholder group that typically holds the most power over a project's direction, the executive stakeholders.

Chapter Five

Executive Stakeholders

The reasonable man adapts himself to the world; the unreasonable one persists in trying to adapt the world to himself. Therefore, all progress depends on the unreasonable man.

George Bernard Shaw

Executive stakeholders launch projects, fund projects, kill projects, and determine when projects are complete. No other group of stakeholders is likely to have as much power over project scope and deliverables as the executive stakeholders. The savvy project manager must develop exemplary skills in managing executive stakeholders.

Who They Are

Executive stakeholders are senior individuals responsible for setting project goals and ensuring the project manager and the project team deliver those outcomes. Executive stakeholders guide, motivate, reinforce, and support the efforts of the project team. Executive stakeholders include the following groups:

- Customer.
- Executive sponsor.
- Executive Council (EC).
- Supplemental executives.

Each of these groups is discussed in more detail in this chapter.

A Word about the Customer

Note that the customer is listed as an executive stakeholder. The customer, arguably, is one of the most powerful stakeholders in the project. The customer approves the project's business requirements at the beginning of a project and determines if those requirements have been achieved at the end of the project. The customer has significant power, just like executive stakeholders, to influence the project goals at the highest level. The project manager should manage the customer using the same techniques deployed when managing executive stakeholders. For all of these reasons, the customer is included in this chapter on executive stakeholders.

The Customer

The individual or group setting the project requirements is the customer. The customer takes a critical role when projects are initiated. In the first phase of the project life cycle, the initiation phase, the customer must define project goals and objectives as clearly and as specifically as possible. During the planning, executing, and monitoring and controlling phases of the project life cycle, the customer should ensure that the project is tracking against the customer's requirements. In the closing phase it is the customer who determines whether the project achieved the desired goals. The project manager should stay in contact with the customer to ensure alignment.

Anticipate the Customer's Needs

Customers need care. They are the reason the project is being done in the first place. Project managers must work diligently to understand the customers and deliver against their goals.

The savvy project manager will understand the customer's larger mission, not just the specific requirements for the project. It is important to learn *why* the customer wants something done in addition to *what* the customer wants to have completed. By understanding why the customer desires certain goals, the project manager will have an increased ability to react quickly to changes in the project.

Executive Sponsor

The primary executive overseeing the project is the executive sponsor. The executive sponsor serves as the project champion and key senior advocate. A strong executive sponsor is important to project success. In some cases there may be multiple executive sponsors. This is discussed in more detail later in this chapter.

Executive Council

The Executive Council consists of senior executives who provide guidance to the project team. The Executive Council should have a representative from each of the major groups or functional areas impacted by the project. A typical Executive Council includes between eight and 16 executives. If the group becomes larger than 16, it is advisable to break the Executive Council into a smaller core group that meets regularly and a supporting group that meets less frequently. It is important that all executives on the core council and in the supporting group stay informed on the project's goals to ensure alignment with overall organizational strategies.

Supplemental Executives

Supplemental executives are defined by who they are not. They are not the executive sponsor, the customer, or part of the Executive Council. Any other executive has the potential to be a supplemental executive. Some supplemental executives will be identified early in the project. They might be in charge of a group that the project touches but is not expected to have a major impact on. Other supplemental executives will emerge as the project advances.

Supplemental executives may be brought into the Executive Council at any time if the project moves into their group or area of responsibility. If the project has a large scope that impacts the entire organization it is wise for the project team to regularly update supplemental executives on project status. Project status updates can be done by the executive sponsor, a member of the Executive Council, or the project manager.

Emergence of a Supplemental Executive

A project team is designing and implementing new roles and responsibilities for all field sales representatives. The project team has a large spreadsheet that identifies all roles and responsibilities for the sales representatives. When the project was initiated, executives from sales, human resources, and operations were included in the Executive Council.

In today's Executive Council meeting the executives decided that 5 percent of the sales representatives' jobs will focus on marketing activities. These activities will be important but a very small part of the sales representative's jobs.

The project manager quickly realizes that the director of marketing is now a supplemental executive. The director does not need to be on the Executive Council because her role is still relatively small, but should be informed about the team's direction and provided the opportunity to give feedback. The project manager promptly adds the director of marketing to the stakeholder register and begins to work on plans to contact the director and bring her into the project.

Note that there may be overlap across these groups. For example, the executive sponsor is likely to serve on the Executive Council. The customer and the executive sponsor may be the same person. A supplemental executive may be promoted to the Executive Council if that executive's area of the organization becomes more involved in the project. Conversely, a member of the Executive Council may shift to a lighter role as a supplemental executive when that member's role on the Executive Council is complete.

Tips for Managing Executive Stakeholders

In this section we discuss tips for managing each of the executive stakeholder groups. In all cases project managers should use their awareness to read the executive environment, and their adaptability to react accordingly. Ideas and perspectives can shift quickly in the executive suite, so the savvy project manager should regularly scan the environment to pick up on any signs of shifts in attitudes toward the project.

Convert Project Language into Executive Language

Executives often have different expectations of the project than the project manager. Where a project manager might talk about earned value, an executive simply wants to know if the project will be done on time and within the budget. Project managers operate in a world of charters, project management plans, work breakdown structures, change control forms, and so on. The executive world is focused on outcomes. Executives want to know what the project will do for the organization. Successful project managers learn how to convert project management language into executive language.

Executives have a lot to keep track of. They are typically not going to have time to invest into gaining the same level of knowledge of project management techniques and terminology as the project manager. The project managers are experts and should consider themselves as such. Project management expertise is accumulated over years of studying, training, and running projects in the real world.

With the exception of executives who spent part of their careers in project management, the typical executive's expertise is likely to be in areas other than project management. Executives are focused on strategic plans, organizational goals, customer deadlines, budgets, and so on. See Table 5.1 for select details on how to convert project language into executive language.

Table 5.1 Convert Project Language into Executive Language

Attribute	What It Means to the Project Manager	How to Describe It to an Executive
Work breakdown structure	A decomposition of the project into the smallest assignable tasks. The key document to feed the project management plan, budget, schedule, and so on.	A planning document that helps the project team ensure that all project work is accounted for and organized.
Project management plan	The primary document used for project planning and execution. Many subplans, such as the quality plan and the scope management plan, feed into the project management plan.	The central document to integrate all aspects of project execution.
Earned value management	A technique to compare budgeted cost of work performed, budgeted cost of work scheduled, actual cost of work performed, and other key project metrics.	An early warning system to identify deviations from the planned time line and budget.
Project charter	A document that formally authorizes the project manager to perform certain tasks and make certain decisions. Typically used as the primary document to launch a new project.	A document to ensure that everyone is in agreement about the project's expected direction and the role of the project manager.
Change request	A formal document that can be a corrective action, preventive action, defect repair, or other adjustment to scope, budget, and so on.	A form used to ensure that all the right people approve project changes and are aware of the changes.

Be Concise

The project manager should be brief, concise, and direct when working with executives. Always have a 30-second so-called elevator speech prepared for the chance executive encounter. The elevator speech should provide a brief synopsis of the project and any specific action(s) the executive can take to help out.

Elevator Speech

The project manager should be ready, at any time, to bump into an executive who wants to know "how it's going." Consider the first example where the project manager does not have a prepared elevator speech:

Kyley (executive): Hi, John. How is your project going?
John (project manager): I'm glad you asked. What a mess. The earned value was on track until two weeks ago. Also, the cost performance index went to 0.9 and we knew we had a problem. We reached out to people and, of course, no one got back to us in time. One person said they did not even know what they were supposed to be doing. Now I'm not sure what's going on. No one seems to want to help around here.

In this example the project manager unloaded a list of problems onto the executive and used project management language instead of executive language. Further, there is nothing actionable for the executive. If the executive wanted to help the project manager, it would not be clear how to do so.

Consider a second example, in which the project manager is prepared for the conversation with a concise, actionable elevator speech.

Kyley (executive): Hi, John. How is your project going?

John (project manager): Good morning, Kyley. Thanks for asking. Overall the project is progressing on track. The schedule looks good. There is one financial item you should be aware of. A recent report showed we are slightly over budget. We caught it early, and I don't think it's going to be a big problem. We're looking into details. I will have more information soon. If you have a few minutes next week, I can stop by and give you a more complete update.

Kyley: Thanks. Please send my assistant a note to schedule the meeting.

In the second discussion the project manager highlighted what was going well in addition to the potential problem with cost. He used executive language and made it clear that the executive did not need to take any action at this point. Also, he planned a concrete next step—a meeting with the executive next week. The project manager has confronted the problem, cost overruns, yet has also shared positive aspects of the project to show that it is not a crisis and that he is confident and firmly in control.

Concise language is essential when working with executives. Brevity is important, too. Executives appreciate communication that is brief and to the point. Also, brevity is important because it implies a higher-level project overview. Most executives, in most situations, will not need to know every detail of the project.

Proactively Identify Problems

Expectations should not be for projects to run perfectly. This is not realistic. The expectation, instead, should be that the project manager proactively identifies problems and quickly takes appropriate actions. Project managers should "run to the problem."

There may be a tendency to shield executives from problems. This is a mistake. Executives are often in a position to help the project team correct problems. The sooner they are aware of the problem, the more options they are likely to have. This does not mean the project manager should go to the executive stakeholders with *every* problem. The successful project manager will use judgment to determine the most important issues for the executive stakeholders.

Understand the Endgame

The project manager should understand *why* a project is being launched, not just *what* must be done. A project team focused only on the "whats" will do fine as long as everything goes according to plan. When something happens that is not planned, however, they will be stuck. The successful project team understands why the project is being launched and the specific goals. The successful project team will have options when something unplanned occurs. Team members will keep their eyes on the goal while determining a different way to get there. The details of their project plan will change but the final destination will not.

Communicate, Communicate, Communicate

Executives like to know the status of the project. They may assume that "no news is good news," but they won't know for sure until the project manager tells them the project status. Even if executives do not ask for status updates, it is a good idea to provide them unless directed otherwise. A routine report with high-level project progress will keep executives informed about the project. The executives may not read every report, but it will be there if they're interested. It will put them more at ease to know they can easily find out how the project is progressing.

This is not only helpful for the executive; it also benefits the project manager. Sharing project updates with executives provides an opportunity for the project manager to solicit feedback on whether the executive stakeholders are happy with the project direction. If the project is moving in a direction that diverges from executive expectations the project manager should know as soon as possible. An early warning means more time to react and a better probability of achieving project success.

Capturing the Hill by a Different Route

Consider the example of a project that is launched to create a flashlight. Two different project teams are given the project to see which team develops the better solution.

Project Team A is determined to capture the project specifications in complete detail. Team A interviews all executive stakeholders and collects what they believe is a comprehensive list of product specifications. The flashlight must be battery powered, it should have an on/off switch, it should be lightweight, and so on.

With these specifications approved and complete, Project Team A commences work to build the new flashlight based on detailed specifications. Several weeks after the project is launched they run into a major problem. They are unable to find an acceptable vendor to produce the body of the flashlight. All vendors are either more expensive than the cost requirements detailed in the specifications or will take longer than the time allotted in the project time line. Team A is stuck.

Project Team B starts off their project by capturing the detailed specifications, just as Team A did. In addition to asking about specifications, however, Project Team B also asks *why* the flashlight is being produced. Team B is told that the company needs to have a lighting device that can be attached to the front of the company's new mining helmets. Team B asks a few more questions and learns that flashlights of this sort can be purchased from a vendor at a lower price than manufacturing them from scratch. Team B recommends flashlights for purchase, and the decision is approved. They have completed their project in one week.

This story shows the difference between focusing on project tasks and focusing on project outcomes. Team B understood the underlying need and came up with a better solution than Team A, which focused only on specifications.

Managing the Executive Council

The Executive Council (EC) is a collection of the project's most active executives. The group should meet on a regular basis to discuss the project. A sample meeting schedule follows:

- *Kickoff meeting.* The first meeting introduces EC members to each other and communicates the project's vision. Ideally, the kickoff meeting occurs before the project is formally launched so EC members have the opportunity to shape the project goals and scope.
- *Status update meetings.* Status updates are routine meetings to share with EC members the key attributes of project performance. Update meetings might include project performance against scope, budget, and time line. Also, update meetings are opportunities to describe any barriers the project team has run into and to discuss strategies to overcome the barriers.
- *Project closeout.* This is a final meeting to ensure that the project has met customer expectations. The final meeting should also be used to capture lessons learned on what went well and what should be improved in subsequent projects.

The project manager is encouraged to meet individually with EC members prior to EC meetings. Pre-meetings become even more critical if the upcoming EC meeting is expected to address challenging issues. In these one-on-one meetings the project manager should provide each EC member with a heads-up that there will be a difficult issue to discuss in the upcoming EC meeting. The project manager should solicit feedback from the EC member and determine if there is a path to resolution that can be executed prior to the meeting. Also, one-on-ones can be used to share a draft version of the EC meeting agenda and determine the level of interest in and sensitivity to each agenda item. This invaluable feedback will help the project manager create an optimized schedule for the EC meeting.

Understand the Executive's Key Drivers

It is important for the project manager to understand the most important issues for each executive. This understanding helps mitigate serious problems in the later phases of the project. The project manager might ask for a brief interview with each executive in the early phases of the project. In this interview the project manager asks questions to get a better understanding of the executive's needs and desires. Examples of questions the project manager can ask to better understand executive stakeholders are:

- What is the most important aspect of this project for you?
- How often would you like to be updated?
- How much detail do you want in the project reports you receive?
- What is the best way to communicate with you (for example, e-mail, telephone, some sort of shared server)?
- What are the watch-outs the project team should be on the lookout for?
- What are your expectations of the project manager? The project team?
- Are there other executives we should talk to about this project?

The project manager, after the initial discussion, should monitor the situation and see if the mutually agreed-upon engagement details are working. If anything does not appear to be working optimally the project manager should approach the executive sponsor and address the situation. The project manager should consider himself or herself the captain of the ship. Any challenges to project success should be addressed quickly.

Build Relationships

Executives, just like project managers, are subject to various forces and pressures. Sometimes these forces are within their control. Many times they are not. The savvy project manager understands that the executives do not have all the answers. Building a relationship with the executives and working with them collaboratively to solve project-related problems

Managing Up: How to Coach Executives on Their Role

If the executive sponsor does not have a lot of experience as a sponsor then the project manager should take time to diplomatically educate the sponsor. Education includes showing the executive sponsor the process the project manager uses to manage projects. This could be a traditional waterfall process, an agile process, or any number of other variations. Showing the executive sponsor, at a high level, the overall process will help the sponsor understand project management and the role a sponsor plays.

The project manager should also have a conversation with the executive sponsor early in the process to ensure clarity on the project goals. The project manager should ask what the executive sponsor expects to get out of the project. Said differently, the project manager should ask, "What does *good* look like?" Some executive sponsors might care most about strict adherence to budget. Other executive sponsors might have a firm time line that is nonnegotiable.

One particularly effective use of executive stakeholders can be to help obtain buy-in. Executive stakeholders have relationships at senior levels of the organization that can facilitate earning support for the project. Executive stakeholders are likely to understand what information and arguments will gain support for the project at executive levels. The smart project manager taps into this knowledge and expertise.

may be a good idea. It is important to note that some executives and some organizational cultures will not welcome the project manager elevating themselves to the level of a partner to the executive. The project manager must use their judgment to gauge what type of relationship they should have with the executive.

Working with Multiple Executive Sponsors

In some cases, a project may have multiple executive sponsors. There are advantages and disadvantages to having multiple executive sponsors.

Advantages of multiple executive sponsors include:

- Each additional executive sponsor will bring to the project team the sponsor's relationships at the executive level. These additional relationships can facilitate buy-in. Additional relationships, however, can also complicate the project, so the project manager must use awareness to determine the impact of each executive's relationships on the project's success.
- Each additional executive sponsor will bring a unique perspective and additional insights that can be leveraged to facilitate project success.
- If one executive sponsor is unavailable at a critical moment when the team requires direction, then the other executive sponsor(s) may be able to field team questions and create resolution in an expedited manner.

Disadvantages of multiple executive sponsors include:

- Potential alignment challenges for the project manager if the executive sponsors disagree with each other.
- Additional stakeholders who must be communicated to in regard to various project updates and details. This can create a scheduling and time consumption burden on the project manager.
- Potential confusion over the project's direction if the multiple executive sponsors are not in close communication with each other.

Be Inclusive

The project manager should welcome additional executives to the stakeholder team. Each new executive is likely to bring knowledge, abilities, and important connections that might help the project succeed. The project manager should attempt to establish a broad coalition of executives in projects to bring the requisite knowledge and support when needed.

Identifying Supplemental Executives

Supplemental executives can be similar to phantom stakeholders (discussed in the next chapter). It is difficult to identify all of them, and, once identified, it may be difficult to discern how to appropriately engage them in the project.

See Chapter 6, Other Stakeholders, for more information on phantom stakeholders.

As projects ebb and flow, the project can move into and out of areas controlled by different executives. The project manager should pay attention to these shifts. When the project moves into a new executive's area of control or expertise, the project manager should consider inviting that executive to be on the Executive Council or to be a supplemental executive. The politically astute project manager will talk with the executive sponsor before making any offers or extending invitations to other executives. In some cases, the project's executive sponsor may decide to extend the invitation on his or her own.

The project may also move away from the area of responsibility or expertise of a particular executive stakeholder. In these situations the project manager should encourage a conversation with the affected executive to determine if participation on the Executive Council is still mutually beneficial.

Watch-Outs

Executive stakeholders typically have more power to influence project direction than other stakeholder groups. Executive stakeholders, among other benefits, can clear obstacles, add expert knowledge, and solicit buy-in during crucial periods. Executives, however, can also block projects or entirely kill them. The project manager must be aware of the key areas where executives and the project team can arrive at cross-purposes with each other. Project managers should be aware of the following watch-outs when working with executive stakeholders.

Time Constraints

Executives, like most project stakeholders, are busy people pulled in multiple directions. The time constraints on executive stakeholders can lead them to disengage from the project. The project manager should find ways to include executives with a minimal time commitment. For example, consider shorter meetings, more concise project-reporting documents, and meetings that are focused on fewer issues so the attendance list can target only the stakeholders tied to those issues.

Disagreements over Jurisdiction

Executives are not always in agreement over who is in control of the different areas impacted by the project. Territorial issues are common, particularly in projects that are cross-functional. Disagreements over jurisdiction can bring projects to a halt and, in some cases, take a long time to resolve due to the sensitivity of the issue. The project manager and the project team should not allow themselves to get too caught up in territorial disputes. These types of debates are typically beyond the control of the project manager and should be addressed with the executive sponsor.

Uninterested

Many organizations suffer from project overload. With so many projects being executed simultaneously, the key stakeholders are likely to focus on the projects they are most interested in. Project managers can keep executives focused on their project by helping them understand why their project is important to the organization's future and to the executive personally. Earlier in this chapter we discussed the importance of the project manager understanding *why* a project has been launched in addition to *what* the project must accomplish. This understanding of organizational importance should be used to help executive stakeholders see the value in the project.

See Chapter 3, Prioritizing Stakeholders, for a useful matrix to prioritize stakeholders according to their level of interest in the project.

Unaware

Time constraints and lack of interest are both contributing factors to a third watch-out for executives—being unaware. Unaware executives do not understand the project's goals or deliverables. This makes them less able to help the project team or speak on its behalf.

The project manager should troubleshoot the reasons behind why the executive is unaware. For example, has the executive missed meetings due to a busy schedule? Is the executive uninterested in the project? Did the team forget to include the executive in the distribution list for meetings? Depending on the root causes, the project manager should develop plans to help the stakeholder become informed on the project.

See Chapter 7, Stakeholder Communication, and Chapter 11, Buy-In, for more detail on how to educate an uninformed executive. Also, see Chapter 3, Prioritizing Stakeholders, for a useful matrix to prioritize stakeholders according to their level of project knowledge.

Micromanager

Certain executives may have a tendency to be *too* involved in the project. We focused, so far, on how to engage executives, inform them, and include them in our projects. All of these skills are important to work with executives who need to be more actively engaged. A different category of executive stakeholder, however, consists of those who should back off. A heavy-handed executive may take over the project and not allow the project team to do its job.

These situations can be sensitive. As with most sensitive executive issues, the project manager is encouraged to solicit the support of the executive sponsor. Working together, the executive sponsor and the project manager can develop strategies to help micromanagers revise their style.

See Chapter 9, Managing Difficult Stakeholders, to learn how to work with challenging executives.

Summary

Executive stakeholders are typically powerful. The project manager should pay close attention to this stakeholder group to ensure that the project is aligned with their expectations. Executive stakeholders include the customer, the executive sponsor, the executives who are on the Executive Council, executives actively involved in the project, and supplemental executive stakeholders who are likely to come and go as the project ebbs and flows.

The project manager should include executive stakeholders in the project, clearly communicate project successes and shortcomings, and always find ways to proactively identify potential barriers to success. We discussed the importance of relationships between the project manager and key executives. Also, it is important for the project's executive sponsor and Executive Council members to have relationships with other project stakeholders to help achieve buy-in and gain alignment around the project's direction.

Executives, like most stakeholders, are busy. We discussed the top watch-outs for working with executive stakeholders. The project manager and project team should constantly be vigilant for ways to make their communications with and engagement of executives concise and efficient.

In Section Two so far we have discussed project team stakeholders and executive stakeholders. In the next chapter, Other Stakeholders, we will discuss external stakeholders, stakeholders subject to the change, and phantom stakeholders.

Chapter Six

Other Stakeholders

The main ingredient of stardom is the rest of the team.

John Wooden

I n the first two chapters in this section we discussed project team members and executive stakeholders. In this chapter we shift our focus to three additional stakeholder groups: external stakeholders, stakeholders subject to the change, and a group we call phantom stakeholders. We discuss each of these stakeholder groups separately, beginning with external stakeholders.

External Stakeholders

External stakeholders are people outside of the project organization who are subject to, part of, or have decision-making power over a project. External stakeholders might include the following groups:

- Vendors.
- Consultants.
- Government regulators.

- Trade unions.
- Associations.
- Not-for-profit groups.
- Citizens' action groups.
- Celebrities.

Clearly, there are many different types of external stakeholders. Next we will discuss tips for working successfully with the external stakeholders most likely to be formally connected to the project—for example, outside vendors and consultants.

Tips for Managing External Stakeholders

Many aspects of managing stakeholders are the same regardless of whether the stakeholder is internal or external. Earning a stakeholder's buy-in, for example, may be equally difficult for internal and external stakeholders. However, there are important differences, too. In this section, we focus on the management areas that are different for external stakeholders.

Establish Contracts . . .

External stakeholders are often connected to the project with a contract. The contract may stipulate the precise terms of the relationship between the external stakeholder and the project. Contract details may include the duration of the stakeholder's involvement, the compensation (if any) the stakeholder will receive for this involvement, and the specific deliverables the external stakeholder is responsible for. Compare this to an internal stakeholder who is an employee of the firm sponsoring the project. The internal employee is not likely to have a formal contract specific to the project, compensation that is tied to the project, an employment duration that is tied to the project, and so on.

Contracts give the project manager and the external stakeholder a definite and written agreement to follow. Well-written contracts are a useful tool to ground both parties on a common understanding. Contracts alone, however, do not manage the relationship. The project manager must establish relationships with external stakeholders.

. . . But Manage Beyond the Contract

The project manager should not rely on the contract alone to define and manage relationships with external stakeholders. It is important to build and maintain an effective working relationship with external vendors. In any project there are likely to be situations that are not covered by the contract language. A good working relationship will help the project manager and the external stakeholder work through the situation together. Also, a working relationship is required to develop buy-in, work through disagreements, and manage any of the myriad of other interpersonal issues that arise in a typical project.

Provide Direction

Many project managers leverage external consultants to assist in projects. External consultants are typically engaged to bring specific subject matter expertise, facilitation skills, experience-based knowledge, and/or process guidance to the project. The project manager should have a direct conversation with the consultant on the overall project mission and the consultant's specific role. The project team, the project organization, and the consultant will all benefit from a clear understanding of the role the consultant will play. This will help maximize the external stakeholder's effort and minimize confusion over roles and responsibilities. Also, consultants with a clear understanding of the endgame are more likely to deliver the desired results.

Hold Outside Vendors Accountable

Outside vendors provide a product or service of value to the project. As with consultants, the project manager should provide direct guidance to the vendor on its role in the project. It is important to be clear on critical project details such as the vendor's scope of work, expected delivery time(s), pricing, and contract acceptance terms. The project manager should check with vendors on a regular basis to ensure performance is meeting the agreed-upon standards.

Getting the Most out of Consultants

A consultant is an expert who applies knowledge, skills, and judgment to a client's situation. There are internal consultants who are employed by the organization they are helping and external or outside consultants who are employed by a consulting firm or some other organization outside of the client.

Consultants are most effective when they have clear direction and understand how to deploy their expertise. The project manager should meet with consultants regularly to ensure alignment between the project team's requirements and the consultant's actions.

External Stakeholders Watch-Outs

External stakeholders must straddle the requirements placed on them by both the project organization and the organization they work for. When these two organizations are at odds, it can lead to stress for the external stakeholder and/or to suboptimal performance. The project manager should pay attention to the external stakeholder's organization to identify when its goals and the project organization's goals are not aligned. When this situation is identified, the project manager should take proactive actions to align the project goals with those of the external stakeholder.

The next external stakeholder group we discuss is the stakeholders subject to the change.

Stakeholders Subject to the Change

Projects create change. Anyone impacted by this change is known as a stakeholder subject to the change. In many projects this represents the largest stakeholder group. The following is a list of several examples of stakeholders subject to the change:

- End users:
  - Individuals using the service(s), product(s), or process(es) created by the project.
  - Others who use project output in any manner.

Caught in the Middle

Catalina, an external consultant, is focused on delivering the best value possible for her client, Nuevo Idea Software. Catalina learns the client's business, interacts with key stakeholders, and works diligently to help Nuevo Idea Software manage a successful project. Nuevo Idea Software is pleased with Catalina's contributions.

Then everything changes. Catalina's employer, Expert Consultants LLC, loses its largest client. Overnight the financial situation at Expert Consultants becomes perilous. Expert Consultants reduces consulting staff. Catalina keeps her job but is required to manage additional clients. Her workload is too heavy and she struggles to keep up.

Catalina begins to spend less time at Nuevo Idea Software. She must work on her other client engagements. Nuevo Idea Software notices that Catalina's contributions are decreasing. The project manager at Nuevo Idea Software becomes concerned.

Catalina is being pulled in two different directions. Her employer, Expert Consultants, is upset when she spends too much time at Nuevo Idea Software, and says she must do a better job managing her time. Nuevo Idea Software, however, says she is not spending enough time with the software firm. Catalina does not know what to do. Does she prioritize the organization paying her every month (Expert Consultants) or the organization that is paying her employer and thereby financing her job (Nuevo Idea Software)? She has relationships at both organizations and does not want to let anyone down. Her frustration grows and her performance declines.

The project manager at Nuevo Idea Software is proactive and recognizes this situation. The project manager seeks conversations with Catalina and the management team at Executive Consultants to figure out a solution. Catalina's reduced effort has become a project risk, and the project manager is determined to find a solution.

- People experiencing changes in their employment status, such as:
  - Gaining a job as a result of the project.
  - Losing a job as a result of the project.
  - Adjustments to a current job as a result of the project, for example, shifting from part-time to full-time, picking up additional responsibilities, or shifting to a new department.
- Members of the community impacted by the project.

Thousands of Stakeholders

Stakeholders subject to the change may be the largest group of stakeholders. Consider a software implementation project. The software, in this example, will be used by 5,000 people across the company's operations. All 5,000 of these people, therefore, are stakeholders because they are subject to the change. Managing this group will be very different from managing a single executive stakeholder or a project team member. Realistically, the project manager will not be able to meet personally with all 5,000 users. Instead, the project manager must manage this group of stakeholders through communication channels such as company newsletters, e-mail, and video teleconferences.

Tips for Managing Stakeholders Subject to the Change

Stakeholders subject to the change will be impacted by the project in some way. The savvy project manager understands how these stakeholders will be impacted and takes actions to help them successfully go through the change. A project team should not impose its will on unwitting stakeholders. Instead, there should be open dialogue and understanding among the project manager, the project team, the project sponsors, and the individuals who are subject to the change.

Many project managers have successfully achieved their project's technical requirements only to see the project fail because the stakeholders subject to the change refused to adopt the new product, service, or process. The project manager's role is to make sure the project is completed and adopted.

Technical Success, Overall Failure

A consumer goods company launches a project to implement a new system the sales force will use to manage customer relationships. A project manager is assigned to the project and the project team is launched. The project team collects all of the detailed technical specifications, including:

- Required fields in the customer relationship system.
- Requirements for reports generated by the system.
- Process work flow requirements.
- Integration guidelines to pull data from existing databases.

After six months of work, the project team announces that all requirements have been met. They claim success and have a celebration party. The new system has been designed, tested, and launched. It appears they have done their job.

Several months after the system goes live, however, there remains a problem—no one is using the system. Not one of the salespeople has switched over to the new system. The project team had decided to leave the current system in place, and everyone is still using it instead of the new system. The sales force does not understand the benefits of the new system, does not see what it can do for them, and does not have any interest in making a change.

This project is an example of a project that met its technical requirements but failed. The project manager must understand what is required to get full adoption from the stakeholders subject to the change and take proactive actions to ensure buy-in from this important stakeholder group.

Explain Why the Project Is Important

Stakeholders who are impacted by the project want to know why the project is important and how it will impact them. They are likely to have many questions about the project, including:

- Why are we doing this project?
- Why is it important to me?
- How will the project impact me?
- How much of my time will it take?

In other words, they are asking, "What does this project mean for me?" The project manager and the executive sponsor must be able to answer these questions and any others that come up from stakeholders subject to the change. It is critical for the project manager to understand the rationale for each project and how it impacts stakeholders subject to the change. In order to ensure that the project manager, the project team, and all other stakeholders in a leadership role are consistent in their message, it may be helpful to create a frequently asked questions (FAQ) document.

Create a FAQ Document

A frequently asked questions (FAQ) document answers the most common stakeholder questions. The project manager, the executive sponsor, and the project team can work together on the FAQ document. This group should identify the key stakeholder concerns and formulate responses.

Typical areas discussed in a FAQ document include:

- How the project will impact people's daily work.
- Why the project is being done in the first place.
- What specific changes people can expect to see as a result of the project.
- Any additional next steps the people can expect from the project.

The FAQ document should be reviewed with key executive stakeholders in advance of communication to a larger audience. This will give executive stakeholders advanced warning on the messaging their team will receive. Also, a preview will provide executive stakeholders the opportunity to give feedback to the project team. The executive stakeholders may identify issues that should be added to the FAQ document or have helpful recommendations on how to word the document in an appropriate manner.

The process of creating this document requires the project team to identify, understand, and respond to stakeholders' primary concerns. The result is a thoughtful document that helps stakeholders understand where the project is going and if and how it impacts them. Also, the FAQ document helps the project manager, the project team, and other project leaders deliver a consistent message about the project.

Be Authentic

It is important for the project manager to be authentic when working with any stakeholder group. This becomes even more important when working with stakeholders subject to the change. These stakeholders will be impacted personally by the project, and therefore pay attention not only to what the project team does but also to how the project team does it. The project manager and the project team must show compassion and understanding through honest, authentic communication.

Solicit Feedback

The successful project manager regularly seeks feedback from the stakeholders subject to the change. The project manager's goal is to ensure that the project is completed and adopted by all stakeholders. This goal cannot be achieved without a deep understanding of the people who will use the project's outcomes. The project manager can deploy several techniques to solicit feedback from stakeholders.

Techniques to solicit stakeholder feedback include:

- Surveys.
- Interviews.
- Focus groups.
- Informal discussions.

The project manager should solicit feedback on an ongoing basis. As the project works through different phases stakeholder opinions may adjust. The savvy project manager has regular communication with stakeholders subject to the change to identify and understand these shifts in opinion and to proactively address them.

Stakeholders Subject to the Change Watch-Outs

Stakeholders subject to the change, in some cases, react differently than other stakeholders. Because the project will impact these people personally, they may have increased sensitivity to project outcomes. This may cause stakeholders subject to the change to be very sensitive to each project message and change in direction. The project manager should be aware of this increased sensitivity and react accordingly.

Appreciate Broad Perspectives

Stakeholders subject to the change can have a wide range of perspectives on the project. Consider the example earlier in this chapter of the group of 5,000 end users impacted by the project. These people may have different levels of experience, different career aspirations, different ways they prefer to receive communication, and so on.

When working with a large group of stakeholders subject to the change, it is important to find the issues that most in the group share—the common denominator. The project manager should focus on these widely shared issues first. Time permitting, the project manager and the project team can take on the more specific issues that may be shared by a smaller number of stakeholders subject to the change. The project manager must use expert judgment to determine how many issues can be addressed. In some cases it may not be reasonably possible to address every stakeholder concern.

Use Clear and Intentional Communication

The savvy project manager develops skills at communicating in a manner that is widely understandable. For example, the project manager should use simple words and should make difficult concepts easy to understand. Also, the project manager should use words that reduce tension instead of words that increase tension. Stakeholders subject to the change may be listening to every word and analyzing it deeply in an attempt to figure out exactly how the project will impact them. Words must be chosen carefully.

See Chapter 7, Stakeholder Communication, for additional guidance on how to communicate effectively with stakeholders.

Use the Adaptability Discipline

Adaptability is one of the six disciplines outlined in the book *A Sixth Sense for Project Management*. The adaptability discipline teaches us that sometimes project managers must adapt to the environment around them. In other situations, however, they must hold firm to their plans. When working with stakeholders subject to the change, the project manager may be under regular pressure to change the project. The savvy project manager deploys the adaptability discipline and change in some situations while feeling comfortable not changing in others.

In the final section of this chapter on other stakeholders we discuss a third group, phantom stakeholders.

Phantom Stakeholders

Phantom stakeholders are people who are subject to, part of, or impacted by the project, yet have not formally been identified by the project manager or project team as stakeholders. Most projects have phantom stakeholders. Over the course of the project, the project manager should identify as many phantom stakeholders as possible. After they have been identified, phantom stakeholders can be formally categorized, prioritized, and managed using the techniques described in other sections of this book. Phantom stakeholders are addressed in this book because they impact project success even though they have not formally been identified as stakeholders.

Identifying Phantom Stakeholders

Before a project manager can manage phantom stakeholders, they must first be identified. In this section we discuss how to do that.

Some project stakeholders, such as the executive sponsor, are easy to identify. Other project stakeholders, however, can be difficult to identify. Phantom stakeholders, by definition, are unidentified and not known to be stakeholders by the project manager or the project team. This creates a challenging situation because these stakeholders are actually impacting the project or have the potential to do so, yet the project manager and the project team are not formally involving them or tracking their activities.

Project managers should go through a regular exercise to identify phantom stakeholders. Several techniques can be used to identify these stakeholders.

Look for Changes in the Project Plan from Unexpected Sources

When change has occurred to the project, such as a scope change, and the initial source of the change is not known, this could be an indicator that there is a phantom stakeholder. The project manager should trace the roots of the project change and discern if there is, indeed, a phantom stakeholder at work.

Look for the Root Causes of Surprises

Surprises are a routine aspect of projects. When a surprise occurs, the project manager should do his or her best to identify the source of the surprise. For example, when the project manager and project team receive surprise information, they should ask themselves if there is someone who knew the surprise information before they did. If this person is not already listed as a stakeholder, the individual should be added to the project stakeholder list.

Look for Discrepancies between Expected Project Execution and Actual Project Execution

It is well-known that things do not always go according to plan in a project. Often, there are good reasons why projects do not progress according to plan. In other cases, the team may not know why the project is delayed. For example, if the project is being delayed in a particular area of the organization, this should be researched. Perhaps there is a phantom stakeholder in that area of the organization who is impacting the project.

In general, the discrepancy between what the project manager expects to happen and what actually happens might indicate that the project manager has a blind spot. Emphasis should be placed on the word *might*. Certainly, there are things that happen in the project environment that cannot be prevented, predicted, or mitigated. However, it is equally true that there are things that happen in a project environment that may come as a surprise to the project manager, but with proper awareness and anticipation should not have been a surprise. Whenever the project manager and project team find themselves in a situation where execution is not going as they expected, then one of the questions they should ask themselves is if there is a phantom stakeholder behind the unexpected problems. If a phantom stakeholder is identified, that person should be added to the project stakeholder register and formally tracked and managed as a project stakeholder.

Ask: "What Is Missing?"

Project managers and project teams are encouraged to ask themselves on a regular basis, "What is missing?" In any project environment there are forces at play, including phantom stakeholders, that can make a very real difference on project outcomes. A project team that actively asks itself, "What is missing?" is more likely to identify these forces. Certainly, there are no guarantees that all forces will be identified. However, asking what is missing increases the probability of identifying phantom stakeholders. This, in turn, increases the probability of project success.

Phantom Stakeholders Are Those Who Have Not Been Identified

It is important to differentiate between phantom stakeholders and identified stakeholders with a limited role. For example, the project manager may be aware of an individual who would like to be more involved with the project. This individual thinks that he is a key stakeholder to the project. However, the project manager and project team may have decided that this individual is not the best person to influence project outcomes.

In this case, the individual in question should be added to the project stakeholder register and managed and tracked as a project stakeholder. This does not mean the team needs to heed the advice of the stakeholder. It simply means the project team is aware of the stakeholder and actively managing and tracking him.

A phantom stakeholder, in contrast, is a stakeholder who has not been identified. Phantom stakeholders are not known to the project team as stakeholders and therefore cannot be managed or tracked. A phantom stakeholder, however, can have a very real effect on the project outcome. That's why it is imperative for the project manager and the project team to ask themselves on a regular basis if there are phantom stakeholders at work. As the project manager and project team identify phantom stakeholders, they should be placed on the project stakeholder register and formally managed and tracked as project stakeholders.

Phantom Stakeholders Watch-Outs

Phantom stakeholders can impact a project in any phase. The project manager should look for phantom stakeholders on an ongoing basis never being content that all stakeholders have been identified.

Project managers must be careful not to confuse phantom stakeholders with the other stakeholder groups. A phantom stakeholder, by definition, is one that the project manager is not aware of. The moment they become identified, they are no longer phantom stakeholders. We use the term *phantom stakeholder* to describe all of the individuals who are influencing our projects without our knowledge. Following the steps listed earlier, the project manager can proactively identify these people and manage them as part of the project.

Summary

In this chapter we discussed three distinct stakeholder groups: external stakeholders, stakeholders subject to the change, and phantom stakeholders. In the previous chapters in this section we discussed project team stakeholders and executive stakeholders. It is helpful to think about project stakeholders in these groupings because stakeholders within a group may have much in common.

External stakeholders include vendors, consultants, and others who are not employed by the project organization. Contracts are often used to set expectations for the specific details of the relationship between external stakeholders and the project team. Contracts, however, are not sufficient alone to manage these stakeholders. The project manager must develop working relationships with external partners.

The next group we discussed is stakeholders subject to the change. Stakeholders in this group will be impacted by the project outcomes. They must be managed carefully and thoughtfully because the stakes are high for this group. The project outcomes may impact their day-to-day responsibilities for years to come.

The third and final group discussed in this chapter is phantom stakeholders. Phantom stakeholders are those that the project manager is not aware of. They can still influence the project in positive and negative ways, though, so the project manager should proactively find phantom stakeholders. Once identified, a phantom stakeholder should be placed on the stakeholder register and managed the same way any other stakeholder would be.

For the remainder of this book we develop general skills that can be applied across all stakeholders. In the next section, Section Three, we shift our focus to managing stakeholder communication and conflict.

Section Three

STAKEHOLDER COMMUNICATION AND CONFLICT

Section Three focuses on project communication and conflict. The section is divided into three chapters: Stakeholder Communication, Managing Stakeholders in a Virtual World, and Managing Difficult Stakeholders.

In Chapter 7, Stakeholder Communication, we focus on different paths to communication success. The successful project manager communicates messages that are clear, consistent, and frequently repeated through multiple communication channels.

In Chapter 8, Managing Stakeholders in a Virtual World, we discuss an area of growing importance, how to work with remotely located stakeholders. Stakeholder management in virtual environments has similarities to and important differences from the in-person environment.

In Chapter 9, Managing Difficult Stakeholders, we discuss techniques for working with stakeholders who present challenges to the project team. Despite the project manager's best efforts, there may still be certain stakeholders who have difficulty working within the construct of the project culture and boundaries. Chapter 9 presents real-world solutions for dealing with these individuals.

Chapter Seven

Stakeholder Communication

He who asks is a fool for five minutes, but he who does not ask is a fool forever.

Traditional Chinese proverb

Communication has occurred when the idea that is in the project manager's head is exactly the same as the idea that is in the project stakeholder's head, and vice versa. Project stakeholder communication is not about getting others to agree with the project manager's idea; that is buy-in and is discussed in a later chapter. Project communication also is not about getting others to follow the project manager. That is leadership, and it is also covered in a later chapter in this book. Project stakeholder communication is focused on ensuring that the concepts and ideas have been correctly understood by all relevant parties. Understanding indicates communication.

Stakeholder Communication Plan

There are a variety of formal project documents that facilitate project communication. Several of the formal documents frequently discussed in project management doctrine include the following:

- Project charter.
- Communications management plan.
- Project stakeholder register.
- Organizational strategic plan.
- Project management plan.
- Gantt charts and other project time lines.

Each of these documents, and many other project documents like them, serves an important communication function. These documents communicate among the relevant stakeholders important aspects of the project. Project documents also facilitate handoffs from one group to another, from one phase of the project to another, and from internal project stakeholders to external project stakeholders. Project documents are often designed with the primary purpose of documenting and communicating the appropriate aspects of the project.

All of these project documents are important. However, alone they do not make up the full body of knowledge and skill set required for effective project communications. There is another layer that must be added to these documents. That layer is focused on project communication channels and the art of communication.

Stakeholder Communication Channels

Communication can occur across many different channels. The project manager should communicate beyond the typical channels of written and spoken words. Communication also involves emotions and nonverbal cues. A partial list of communication channels includes the following.

- Verbal:
  - In person.
  - On the phone.
  - Via online and mobile technologies.

- Nonverbal:
  - Facial expression.
  - Body language.
  - Gestures.
- Written:
  - Electronic.
  - Notepads or paper.
  - Whiteboards and SMART Boards.
- Visual:
  - Charts.
  - Graphs.
  - Pictures or images.
- Kinesthetic or experiential:
  - Hands-on training.
  - Case studies.
  - Active simulations of project tasks.

Verbal Stakeholder Communication

Verbal communication is the use of spoken words to send messages. Speaking with each other is an excellent way for the project manager and project stakeholder to discuss sensitive or difficult-to-understand project attributes. Whereas written communication can be used for updates and sharing data, verbal communication is desired if the project manager and the stakeholder need to talk through a situation where the best answer is not obvious.

Advantages of Verbal Communication

Verbal communication can be a very effective way to work through differences. Verbal communication allows real-time give-and-take between two or more parties. Each party can offer thoughts and ideas and the other party can react to them.

The most effective verbal communicators use their words to create images and stories. Painting a picture with words is a very effective way to engage stakeholders. Instead of simply reading through data and technical details, project managers who can tell stories with the data and create visual imagery with the data have a higher probability of communicating their points and keeping their audience engaged.

Disadvantages of Verbal Communication

Verbal communication does have some disadvantages. One disadvantage, because verbal communication is in real time, is that it may put project managers in a position where they are asked questions they are not prepared to answer. Also, like any form of communication, misunderstandings can occur if the project manager uses an abstract word or phrase. Different words and phrases can take on new meanings in different cultural settings.

When communicating, the project manager should be careful to select language that is simple and easy to understand. When talking to a general audience that is not familiar with project management the project manager should avoid using technical project management phrases, acronyms, and any language that would not be considered part of the vocabulary of a typical seventh-grade student.

Nonverbal Communication

When two people communicate in person much of the communication occurs nonverbally. Interestingly, most project managers have little training on nonverbal communication. Seasoned project managers may have been coached at some point in their careers on verbal communication and written communications. It is far less likely that they have received coaching on how to sit in meetings, how to stand to show authority, and so on. However, project managers should be encouraged to put themselves on a course of study that enables them to improve their nonverbal communication. Also, it is important for the project manager to send out communication messages verbally and nonverbally that are consistent with each another. For example, the project manager should not smile while delivering difficult news.

Advantages of Nonverbal Communication

Nonverbal communication, when used effectively, is a powerful way to get one's point across. When used in concert with verbal communication, nonverbal communication can reinforce the message. For example, tone of voice, facial expression, word selection, and speed of speech are all components of nonverbal communication. These nonverbal components help communicate the project manager's underlying attitudes and feelings in addition to the overt verbal message. This is valuable in showing the project manager's confidence, enthusiasm, and optimism about the project.

Disadvantages of Nonverbal Communication

Perhaps the biggest disadvantage of nonverbal communication is that it is frequently misunderstood. People may make assumptions when they see a certain nonverbal behavior. The project manager should be aware of nonverbal behavior but must be careful not to draw incorrect conclusions from it. As with verbal communication, nonverbal communication is subject to cultural and individual differences. A gesture in one culture might mean something very different in another culture. There are cultural differences in nonverbal meeting etiquette. These differences can be found across a broad range of areas, including whether to shake hands, the appropriate amount of eye contact, and the proper amount of personal space granted during an in-person conversation. In Western cultures direct eye contact is perceived as an indication of confidence and a positive attitude. In Eastern cultures, however, direct eye contact may be unwelcome.

Crossed Arms

What does it mean when someone crosses their arms? Some argue that crossed arms indicate a closed body position. In a closed body position, the argument goes, people are physically closing themselves off to ideas by using their crossed arms to block their body and show they are not interested. It is dangerous, however, to draw absolute conclusions from this nonverbal behavior.

Stakeholders may cross their arms because they are cold. Crossed arms might be a habit. An individual may have injured an elbow and found that crossing the arms relieves the pain in the elbow. There are many different reasons why people might cross their arms.

See Chapter 11, Buy-In, for more details about nonverbal communication.

Written Stakeholder Communication

Excellent writers use the power of written communication to get their point across. Clear writing, however, may be challenging to those who are not experts. Sentence structure, word choice, and a variety of other technical aspects of writing all contribute to the degree to which the writing communicates ideas. As we discussed, communication is about making sure the idea the project manager has in his or her head is the same as the idea in the stakeholder's head. The goal of written communication in a project environment is to share ideas in a manner that is understandable.

Advantages of Written Communication

Written communication enables skilled writers to be precise in how they communicate their ideas. Project managers can take time to communicate their message using exactly the words they desire. If done properly, this increases the precision of writing as a communication channel. Also, writing transcends time. Through technologies such as e-mail or shared documents the project manager can write a message that the stakeholders can view at their convenience. Real-time verbal communication, of course, requires both parties to be engaged at the same time.

Disadvantages of Written Communication

One of the downsides of written communication is that it does not show nonverbal communication such as tone of voice, facial expression, and intonation. For example, a project manager may send an e-mail to a project stakeholder that includes a joke. The project stakeholder may not understand that the content is a joke and may instead interpret the e-mail in a different way than was originally intended. This could lead to miscommunication or, even worse, a conflict. Project managers are discouraged from using any type of humor, sarcasm, or colloquialism that might be misinterpreted or misunderstood. In particular, this is important with project stakeholders with whom the project manager does not have a personal relationship. Stakeholders with a personal relationship with the project manager are more likely to understand the underlying meaning of the words.

Visual Communication

Visual communication includes images, charts, graphs, and any variety of tools used to visually display project information. The project manager should find ways to communicate key project time lines and deliverables in a visual manner. Different people have their own preferred method of receiving communication. Some people prefer conversations and others prefer information in writing using words; in contrast, others respond best to pictures, charts, and graphs. Project managers are encouraged to use visual communication as a routine part of their communication strategy.

Advantages of Visual Communication

Certain stakeholders are likely to understand visual communication better than other forms of communication. Adults process information in a variety of different ways depending on the individual. Some adults are visual, others are auditory, others prefer written language, and so on.

Visual imagery can communicate some information more succinctly than words. We all know the saying "A picture is worth a thousand words." Visual imagery should be used to complement written and verbal messages.

Disadvantages of Visual Communication

As we have discussed, any type of communication can be misunderstood, and visual communication is no different. When using visual communications, the project manager should clearly label all charts and all parts of the chart such as the axes, data sets, and sources. The project manager is encouraged to share visual communication with several reviewers before sending it out to a larger group. The project manager should ask the reviewers what key points are communicated to them from viewing the visual communication. This is an effective cross-check to ensure that the visual communication is transferring the desired ideas.

Kinesthetic Communication

Kinesthetic communication is characterized by showing people what to do and then providing them an opportunity to do it themselves. The other communication channels we discussed in this chapter are focused on explaining how to do something. The kinesthetic communication channel, by contrast, is focused on guiding individuals to learn on their own by actually doing the activity themselves. This can be one of the most effective ways to communicate. In the prior section we repeated the well-known saying "A picture is worth a thousand words." With kinesthetic learning we can create a new saying: "A hands-on experience is worth a thousand e-mails."

Learning by Doing

A project manager in a manufacturing company is meeting with several executive stakeholders. The project is suffering delays due to a manufacturing problem. The project manager is using verbal communication to explain to the executives the challenges the team is experiencing with the manufacturing operation.

"There are two pieces coming out of different manufacturing facilities that need to be put together," the project manager explains. "The plant employees are having a difficult time getting these two pieces to snap together. The two pieces have different patterns."

The executive stakeholders gaze uncertainly at the project manager. They know there is a problem but do not understand why the pieces don't fit together. The project manager realizes that this is an ideal opportunity for kinesthetic communication. He runs back to his office and grabs the two pieces being discussed. He returns to the meeting room and hands them to the executive stakeholders.

"Here, try to fit them together," the project manager says.

Immediately, the executive stakeholders understand the problem. By seeing and doing they have learned. The kinesthetic communication style has succeeded in getting the point across.

Communicating through Emotions

Emotions are a powerful communication tool. Research shows that people are more likely to remember experiences that have an emotional component to them.[1] This phenomenon surely happens in a project environment as well. If project stakeholders have an emotional reaction to something that happens in the project, they are more likely to remember it. The savvy project manager understands this and is thoughtful about the emotional aspect of all team communications and interactions.

Training with Emotion—A Personal Note from the Author

I recall a case study from business school years ago. In this case study the group I was in was required to make a decision. We did not have all of the information, nor did we have as much time as we wanted, but the decision was required. It turned out the case study was based on a real-world sequence of events. The decision we had made as a group was the same decision made in real life. That decision had unfortunate consequences. I recall how I felt emotionally after completing the case study. Even now, more than 10 years after completing the case, I remember the emotions I felt going home from class that evening.

That emotional response led me to change some of my decision-making behaviors. True learning had occurred. From this experience I saw firsthand the power of emotions and learning. Roeder Consulting now uses case studies and exercises in several of its classes that evoke similar feelings. Although not always a fun experience, the emotions attached with the learning ensure that the conscientious student will remember the experience, and its lessons, forever.

---

[1] Elizabeth A. Kensinger, "Remembering Emotional Experiences: The Contribution of Valence and Arousal," *Reviews in the Neurosciences* 15 (2004): 241–252.

The project manager should understand that an emotional meeting may leave a lasting impact on the stakeholders. The stakeholders may be more likely to remember that the meeting was emotionally difficult, even if they don't remember the exact details of what made it so. This goes back into the category of awareness. Each project, each stakeholder, and each project manager is different. There is no single cookie-cutter approach that can be applied to all communication. The project manager who is more aware of the different methods of communication and the emotional impact of these methods is more likely to have successful project outcomes.

Holistic Communication

The project manager is hosting a meeting with key project stakeholders. She shares a written document with the project time line. While stakeholders view the document, the project manager speaks about a few of the key tasks and milestones. She is using verbal and written communication styles. However, the project manager's awareness is telling her that the key points are not getting across.

The project manager decides to share a Gantt chart showing the time line and key milestones in a visual format. She is deploying visual learning in addition to verbal and written learning. She can see the stakeholders quickly understand the Gantt chart, and her ideas have been communicated.

By deploying all three of these communication channels simultaneously—verbal, written, and visual—the project manager has greatly increased the chances of proper communication with the project stakeholders.

Again, communication is about transferring thoughts and ideas in a way so they are understood. Understanding indicates communication.

Holistic Approach to Communication

The savvy project manager holistically deploys all of the different communication channels addressed in this chapter. Reality may dictate that the project manager must use one channel, such as written communication, disproportionately. The project manager, however, should constantly and creatively seek various channels for use to communicate the message. In addition to using different communication channels, the project manager should repeat the message.

Repetition facilitates learning. Small children often enjoy watching the same television show over and over. This helps them learn. Adults benefit from repetition too. The project manager should not be afraid to say the same thing over and over until it is certain that stakeholders understand the key concepts. One technique is to lead all meetings with a brief statement of scope for the project. After seeing and hearing the statement of scope many times, the project stakeholders will be able to recall the purpose of the project.

Summary

In summary, project stakeholder communication is part science and part art. The main point of this chapter is that there are many different types of communication: verbal, nonverbal, written, visual, kinesthetic, and emotional. The most effective communicators learn how to use these communication channels holistically. Since poor communication has been the cause of failure for so many projects the savvy project manager embraces the holistic approach to communication.

It is also important to be persistent in the communication of the message. Successful project managers communicate the same message to their stakeholders over and over. It takes repetition for the message to sink in. Repetition also serves the purpose of reinforcing the message and demonstrating that the project manager and the project team fully intend to execute their plan. Verbal, written, and visual communication channels should be deployed consistently to communicate the same message in multiple ways. In some cases, kinesthetic and emotional learning may also be deployed by the project manager to facilitate an even deeper level of communication. As always, project managers should use their awareness of their stakeholders and the situation to get feedback on the degree of success they're having in communicating key project information.

Project documents such as the project management plan provide written information about the project. Alone, these documents are not sufficient to communicate key project goals and ideas to stakeholders. The project manager must understand the technical documents used to track and manage communication, but should not use them as the entire communication strategy. Personal contact is required.

The successful project manager realizes that communication is a two-way street and is constantly open to communication from their stakeholders. The project manager should ask clarifying questions and ensure that they understand the message being communicated to them. It is never a good idea to make assumptions and to assume understanding. If there is ever any doubt the project manager should ask clarifying questions to ensure a common level of understanding among project manager, project team, and project stakeholders.

Many stakeholders may work in a different location from each other, from the project manager, and from the project team. This geographic dispersion can make communication more challenging. In the next chapter, Managing Stakeholders in a Virtual World, we discuss how to communicate with and manage stakeholders virtually.

Chapter Eight

Managing Stakeholders in a Virtual World

Whoever invented the meeting must have had Hollywood in mind. I think they should consider giving Oscars for meetings: Best Meeting of the Year, Best Supporting Meeting, Best Meeting Based on Material from Another Meeting.

William Goldman

Project work is increasingly becoming virtual work. Organizations are becoming more global. More people are working from home. Mobile technology is prevalent. All of these forces are contributing to an increase in virtual project teamwork. Project stakeholders may be in different time zones, different locations, different countries, or any other variety of situations that leads to the need for virtual meetings. Working and meeting with stakeholders in a virtual environment creates a unique set of challenges. It also creates benefits.

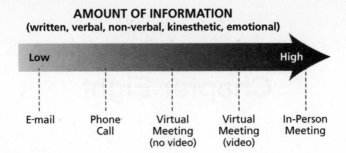

AMOUNT OF INFORMATION
(written, verbal, non-verbal, kinesthetic, emotional)

Low   High

| E-mail | Phone Call | Virtual Meeting (no video) | Virtual Meeting (video) | In-Person Meeting |

Figure 8.1 Continuum of Robustness
© 2012 Roeder Consulting.

The Continuum of Robustness

Virtual meetings should be conducted in the most robust method. The project manager's goal in a virtual environment is to select the method that deploys as many of the communication channels discussed in Chapter 7 as possible. The most robust methods enable all of the different communication channels to be engaged: verbal, nonverbal, written, visual, kinesthetic, and emotional.

Figure 8.1 shows the most robust methods on the right, the least robust methods on the left, and moderately robust methods in the middle. When communicating key points, the project manager should start at the right of the continuum and ask, "Can I schedule an in-person meeting?" If possible, this is the most robust method and should be selected. There may be opportunities for in-person meetings even if most of the project work is conducted virtually. When budgets are tight, in-person meetings can be scheduled around other events that may bring all stakeholders to a single location.

In Person

On the far right side of the continuum of robustness is the in-person meeting. As discussed, the in-person meeting is the best way to build team relationships and team trust. In virtual teams it may be difficult, or impossible, to bring together all stakeholders for in-person meetings.

The Annual Trade Show

Project managers should constantly look for ways to bring their team together. Sometimes, this can be accomplished by piggybacking team meetings on top of in-person events that are scheduled for other reasons. One example is the annual trade show. If a large number of the project's stakeholders will be in attendance, the project manager can organize a gathering. The gathering does not need to be a business meeting. The scheduled interaction can be a social gathering to allow stakeholders to build relationships and learn more about each other. Even if the project manager is not able to personally attend the show, he or she can organize ways for key stakeholders to connect.

The project manager should seek ways to meet in person with as many stakeholders as possible.

In-person meetings, as shown in Table 8.1, provide an opportunity to use all communication channels: verbal, nonverbal, written, visual, kinesthetic, and emotional. It is important to note that Table 8.1 shows the communication channels *possible* within a given method. It is up to the project manager to actively design ways to deploy as many of these channels as applicable.

Virtual Technology with Live Streaming Video

There are a variety of virtual meeting platforms commonly available that offer live streaming video, sharing of slides and other visual matter, and an audio connection. Project teams using this technology are able to share information using all of the different communication channels, although some of the channels have less robustness than possible in person. Also, these technologies may provide powerful audio capabilities to the host, such as the ability to mute select microphones if there is

Table 8.1 Communication Channel Availability

	Verbal	Nonverbal	Written	Visual	Kinesthetic	Emotional
In person	Yes	Yes	Yes	Yes	Yes	Yes
Virtual with live streaming video	Yes	Partial	Yes	Yes	Partial (create scenario for hands-on experience)	Partial (more difficult to create emotional experience remotely)
Virtual without video	Yes	Vocal nonverbal only	Yes	Yes	Partial (create scenario for hands-on experience)	Partial (more difficult to create emotional experience remotely)
Audio only (e.g., phone call)	Yes	Vocal nonverbal only	Yes—send in advance	Yes—send in advance	Partial (create scenario for hands-on experience)	Partial (more difficult to create emotional experience remotely)
Written only (e.g., e-mail)	—	—	Yes	Yes	Minimal (describe hands-on experience to be done on own)	Partial (emotions must be created through written words; possible only for excellent writers)

excessive background noise from one of the participants that is disruptive to the meeting.

Nonverbal cues such as facial expressions and tone of voice are communicated in a virtual platform with live streaming video. This technology also typically enables written and visual documents to be shared. In some cases, the project manager may choose to send out these documents in advance. Some of the virtual platforms enable real-time editing of documents, with any of the virtual team members typing their comments into the live screen and sharing feedback in real time.

The project manager must be creative to deploy kinesthetic and emotional communication using a virtual platform. The project manager must plan in advance a scenario for hands-on learning for kinesthetic communication, and also scenarios for emotional communication. In some cases, the project manager can facilitate kinesthetic or emotional communications in a virtual environment by sending advance materials that will be used in the virtual meeting.

See Chapter 7, Stakeholder Communication, for more details on the communication channels.

Virtual Technology without Video

Virtual technologies that do not include live streaming video are typically able to do all of the items mentioned in the preceding section with the exception of video. The facilitator should be able to share documents in real time and edit them in the platform. In many technologies the participants, with the facilitator's approval, also have the ability to share documents and make real-time edits. In addition, the audio bridge may provide the facilitator the opportunity to mute microphones as necessary. With the absence of video, a portion of nonverbal communication is lost, leading to a less robust communication channel.

Audio Only

When in-person meetings and virtual technologies are not an option, the next best option available to project managers is to use audio only. Audio communication can be achieved using online technologies, mobile technologies, or traditional landline telephones. Verbal communication, of course, is maintained in meetings that are audio only. Also, contrary to what many may believe, there is still some nonverbal communication available in an audio meeting. Tone of voice, voice volume, and speaking speed are all components of nonverbal communication that are discernible from audio. Project managers accustomed to working in an audio-only virtual environment may become skilled at picking up these vocal cues and understanding how to interpret them.

Written and visual documents can also be used in audio-only meetings. The project manager has the option of either sending documents in advance or sending them during the meeting. Kinesthetic and emotional experiences can be created in audio with some creativity.

Written Only

Written communication is the least robust method to deploy for virtual teams. As demonstrated in Table 8.1, written communication does not deploy all six communication channels. This places extreme emphasis on quality of writing to get the point across. When using written communication, the project manager loses the ability to verbally explain ideas, and also loses all nonverbal information.

When working in a virtual environment, research shows that written communication is the least effective way to build trust with stakeholders.[1] Written communication in a virtual environment may be seen as less personal. The project manager should constantly strive for ways to build relationships within the team. With this goal in mind, the project manager should use communication channels as far to the right as possible on the continuum of robustness.

---

[1]Shawn Adderly, "Technology Not Always the Best Tool for Communication," University of Illinois research discussed in the *Daily Illini*, August 3, 2012.

Risks of Virtual Teams

Virtual teams create additional risks for the project manager. As with any risk, the project manager can effectively decrease the probability of the virtual risk by proactively identifying and managing it.

Risks of working in virtual teams include:

- Failure of audio or video technology.
- Time zone differences.
- Distractions in the environment of the virtual team member.
- Cultural differences.
- Different country-specific or region-specific laws and regulations.
- Language barriers.

Several of these risks are discussed in more detail in the following subsections.

Technology Risks

The project manager should have a backup plan for virtual meetings. What will be done if the Internet connection is dropped? What if the presenter loses cell phone coverage? What if a participant's computer shuts down in the middle of the meeting? The savvy project manager thinks through the most probable technology failures prior to the meeting and establishes guidelines on how to react in the event that failure occurs.

Time Zone Risks

Global project teams often have difficulty finding times that are suitable to all stakeholders. When working with stakeholders across different time zones the project manager should consider varying the meeting times. Meeting times should be determined so they are convenient for each of the different stakeholders on a rotating basis.

Backup Technology and People

Duplicate technology can reduce the risk of technology-related failures in virtual meetings. When using an online virtual technology platform, one technique is to use one platform for visual communications and a separate conference calling number for audio communications. If the Internet fails, there will still be an audio line. If the phone line fails, there will still be a visual communication tool for sending notes and other information.

Another option is for the facilitator to use two computers when on virtual meetings. If the first computer loses its connection or fails to work in any way, the facilitator can switch to the second computer and seamlessly continue with the meeting.

In addition to backing up systems, it is advisable to back up presenters. The savvy facilitator sends the presentation to one or two team members prior to the meeting. If the facilitator loses the connection, then the other team members can pick up where the facilitator left off by following the documentation sent to them in advance.

There is a positive aspect to the distributed nature of virtual meetings. Virtual meetings create a redundancy that can actually mitigate risks that can't be mitigated when meeting in person. For example, if the power goes out in the building where an in-person meeting is being held, then everyone in that meeting is impacted. In a virtual meeting, however, a power failure in one area impacts only a select group of people. Everyone else can continue with the meeting.

Miscommunications on meeting times are common in a virtual environment. Stakeholders may have difficulty converting the meeting time in the e-mail or meeting invitation into their local time. Some geographies have a time zone that is offset from Greenwich Mean Time by 30 minutes instead of one hour. Also, some geographies shift their time with daylight saving time whereas others do not. To mitigate

Varying Time Zones

Project managers in global projects should consider moving around meeting times. For example, in the first week of the project, the project manager might select an evening time in the U.S. eastern time zone, which would be early morning for stakeholders in Asia. In week two, the project manager might select a midmorning meeting time in the U.S. eastern time zone to allow European stakeholders to join the meeting before heading out for dinner. By rotating the meeting times, the project manager can build team cohesion by providing each geography with the courtesy of a convenient meeting schedule at least some of the time.

As part of the meeting agenda development, the project manager should also be careful to create agendas that require the meeting's biggest issues to be directed by the geography with the convenient meeting time for that meeting. In other words, if the next scheduled meeting is going to require extensive input from the Brazilian office, then schedule that meeting at a time that is convenient for Brazil. This will help the Brazilian team be at their best for their presentation. Also, this strategy can provide an opportunity for other geographies less impacted by the issues on the meeting agenda to opt out of the meeting if they wish.

misunderstandings, the project manager is encouraged to show the meeting time in the most common time zones stakeholders will participate from. This extra effort for the project manager can make a significant difference in meeting attendance rates.

Virtual Distractions

Distractions can lead to suboptimal virtual meetings. In certain cases, serious distractions can bring virtual meetings to a halt. Project teams should establish a protocol on how to handle distractions in the

Mute That Microphone!

Each environment has its own unique sounds. A person in a meeting room might hear chairs creaking, hands tapping on the table, and air vents blowing into the room. A person sitting at a coffee table at home might hear birds chirping outside the window, barking dogs, or the doorbell ringing. Someone in an airport will hear flight announcements and the drone of voices, squeaky bag wheels, and heels on linoleum floors. Put all of these sounds together and it makes a virtual meeting.

Facilitators of virtual meetings are encouraged to ask participants to mute their microphones when they are not talking. The facilitator should keep in mind that participants may require a few moments to unmute their microphones if they want to talk. The facilitator should pause long enough for people to unmute and talk before proceeding to the next topic.

In some situations the background noise in a given environment may wash out people's voices when they unmute their microphones and attempt to speak. Encourage these people to keep their microphones muted and instead participate by adding their comments into the text box or some other written format available in the virtual platform. Although written communication is a less robust communication channel than verbal communication, it is far better than an eardrum-splitting racket from the background noise.

virtual environment. Protocols, at minimum, should address the following issues:

- How to minimize background noise (for example, mute microphones).
- How to allow everyone a chance to speak (for example, pause five seconds before moving to the next topic).

- How to work through disagreements (for example, take conversations offline if they are between two people and taking more than three minutes of team time in the meeting).
- How to manage time zones (for example, regularly switching meeting times).
- How to manage technology failures (for example, establishing a backup plan for various technology-related risks).

Cultural Differences

The project manager should do homework on the cultural differences of the individuals in the team. Cultural differences impact many areas, including decision making, verbal and nonverbal communication norms, and the amount of time spent talking versus listening. A few examples are offered later in the chapter. It is important for project managers to understand these differences, and not to apply their personal cultural attitudes on communication toward all stakeholders in the project.

Geographic Diversity

Virtual teams are likely to be geographically dispersed. Geographic diversity might mean that there are different regional laws and regulations. The project manager should understand how these regional laws and regulations impact the project. If necessary, the project manager's legal department should be included as a project stakeholder.

Each geography also presents its own unique set of weather characteristics, holidays, back-to-school dates, and so on. Early in the project the project manager should ask stakeholders to list key dates and events in their area. These events should be entered into a master calendar used to scheduled team meetings and deliverables.

In-Person Communication Has Risks, Too

Many of the risks just mentioned can also occur in an in-person environment. These risks, however, can be exacerbated in a virtual environment. For example, language barriers can be more readily overcome in person with the use of hand gestures, images, or nonverbal communication. In a virtual environment it is more difficult to simulate these methods of communication. This is one more reason why the project manager should select a meeting method that is as robust as possible.

Virtual Fairness

Some organizations are creating rules for virtual meetings. These rules are intended to make virtual meetings fair for all participants so no single stakeholder or group of stakeholders benefits from an advantage.

In one organization the leadership decided it was not fair for a group of people to be in a room together while others were using their telephones to dial in to the meeting. They observed that the people in the room would get into conversations with each other and not provide an opportunity for persons on the phones to talk. Also, printed documents were shared in the meeting room that the phone participants had not seen before.

As a response to this imperfect situation, the organization created a policy stating that if one person is required to meet virtually, then everyone is required to meet virtually. People in the same office space are now required to sit at their desks and use virtual technology to talk with each other and the outside participants. This policy, it is argued by the leadership team, creates a level playing field for all participants.

Opportunities When Working Virtually

Working with stakeholders in a virtual environment also creates opportunities that may not be present if all stakeholders are in one location. These opportunities, if harvested by the project manager, increase the probability of project success.

Select opportunities from working in virtual teams include:

- A richness in insight and perspective that comes from a diverse group of stakeholders.
- Ability to time-phase project work where stakeholders from different time zones can be deployed in an organized manner. This may enable the project team to get more work done in a 24-hour period than they would be able to accomplish otherwise.
- Ability to deploy virtual tools, such as polling, during stakeholder meetings.
- Ability to record stakeholder meetings to the advantage of stakeholders unable to attend.

These opportunities are discussed in more detail in the following subsections.

Diverse Group of Stakeholders

Virtual teams can bring stakeholders with rich and vibrant experiences. The very same language and cultural differences that may hinder communication can at the same time enhance the variety of perspectives used to analyze a project. As the number of cultures, time zones, languages, and so on in a stakeholder group increases, so does the diversity and breadth of knowledge and experience. The savvy project manager will tap into these diverse experiential bases to the advantage of the project.

Leveraging Multiple Time Zones

Project teams with stakeholders in multiple time zones may be able to get more work done in a 24-hour period. Work can be passed from project team members in one time zone to team members in the next. In some cases where project team stakeholders are located around the world the work may progress continuously. This provides a real advantage in getting projects completed quickly.

Successfully executing around-the-clock project work requires clear expectations and crisp communication. The members of the team must understand their roles and the handoffs between their work and the work of other team members. Technology such as shared servers and common work sites can enhance the communication.

See Chapter 7, Stakeholder Communication, for more information on how to create effective team communication.

Leveraging Virtual Tools

Many virtual meeting tools commonly available for use on the Internet have polling technologies. The virtual polling technology has more precision than simply asking a large group of people to raise their hands and will immediately count the percentage of people voting for each choice. In addition to the polling technology, many virtual meeting tools include the ability to chat and other forms of written communication. Participating stakeholders can send informative notes to each other without distracting the larger group.

Although this written technology can have the downside of enabling side conversations it can also have the added benefit of enabling individual stakeholders to ask another stakeholder a question that may not be relevant for the group. During in-person situations it is common for one person to have a question that the other stakeholders already know the answer to. If the other stakeholders must sit and wait while the person's questions are answered it is not a productive use of their time. The smart project manager can take advantage of virtual technology to have these questions answered on the side without delaying the rest of the team. The project manager may select someone on the team to monitor the chat panel and respond to questions while the project manager facilitates the overall meeting.

Recording Meetings

Many commonly available virtual meeting rooms also provide the opportunity to record meetings. Recording the virtual meeting enables stakeholders who cannot attend the meeting to educate themselves on the meeting content at a later date. This can be a very powerful tool given today's increasingly busy workforce.

Summary

In summary, a variety of forces are leading to the increased use of virtual teams. Project managers leading virtual teams should use the continuum of robustness to ensure they are using the most robust method possible. The continuum of robustness, combined with the lessons in the previous chapter on communication, work together to provide the project manager effective techniques for managing virtual teams.

Virtual teams create risks. Technology risks, language differences, time zone differences, and a variety of other risks can derail the virtual team. As with any project risk management strategy, the successful project manager should proactively identify risks and develop plans to mitigate them.

Virtual teams also create opportunities. The exciting development of new virtual technologies enables project teams to do things today they could not have done in the recent past. The project manager should embrace these opportunities and work with the project team to develop new and creative ways to take advantage of new technologies.

Projects create change. Despite the project manager's best efforts at clear communication and competent team leadership, there may still be conflict and difficult stakeholders. In the next chapter we will discuss how to manage these difficult stakeholders.

Chapter Nine

Managing Difficult Stakeholders

If you are going through hell, keep going.
Winston Churchill

Seasoned project managers, when asked what is most difficult about managing projects, will most commonly respond that it's the "people issues." Each issue is an opportunity for the project manager to take a leadership role and drive change.

The project manager's goal, first and foremost, is to deliver project success. The path to success is not a straight line. Some stakeholders embrace the project scope, whereas others do not. Those who resist are not necessarily wrong. They may simply have a different viewpoint or set of experiences. The project manager must stay open-minded when dealing with difficult stakeholders and work diligently to understand the root causes that are leading a stakeholder to be difficult.

Projects Create Tough Issues

Project management, by definition, is focused on creating something new. When creating something new, it should be expected that the standard-bearers of the status quo will question the changes. Many projects may find success without major disagreement. Other projects, however, may result in significant levels of anxiety and disagreement. In these situations it is not unusual for the project manager to be thrust into the middle of difficult situations.

Project managers should not feel as though they are doing something wrong if the project environment is characterized by disagreement. Projects often handle tough issues that must be dealt with but that are not easy. The nature of change can lead to anxiety. The successful project manager understands this and views project disagreements as opportunities to display the manager's well-rounded project tool kit, which includes the ability to deal with challenging situations.

Categorizing Difficult Stakeholders

Earlier in this book, in Chapter 2, we discussed categories for stakeholders. Building on this theme, we now discuss how to categorize the difficult stakeholders. When dealing with difficult stakeholders, it is important for the project manager to know which of two groups the stakeholder falls into:

1. Difficult stakeholder whose support is "nice to have."
2. Difficult stakeholder whose support is a "must have."

It is best, of course, to have everyone's support. In some cases, however, this may not be possible. The project manager must understand where support is required.

Difficult Stakeholders Who Are Optional for Project Success

For the purposes of this chapter, we divide project stakeholders into two groups. The first group is stakeholders who are optional for project success. By definition, the support of these stakeholders is not required for the project to move forward. The project manager may desire their support and feel more comfortable with their support; however, if absolutely necessary, the project manager is able to proceed without it. This is important to keep in mind when dealing with a difficult stakeholder optional for project success. It is important because the project manager can work with the other, supportive stakeholders and proceed without the support of the difficult stakeholder.

When following the steps outlined later in this chapter, the project manager should do his or her best to work with the difficult stakeholder but is not required to work with the stakeholder if it becomes too challenging to do so. The project manager should solicit the support of the executive sponsor in enabling the project manager to move forward with those stakeholders who are supportive.

It is important to note that some difficult stakeholders indicate they are required for project success even if they are not. It is incumbent on the project manager to determine if the difficult stakeholder is truly required for project success.

Difficult Stakeholders Who Are Required for Project Success

Project managers must find a way to work with difficult stakeholders who are required for project success. If a given stakeholder has the ability to stop or derail a project, then the project manager must form a working relationship with this stakeholder no matter how difficult. The following process increases the project manager's success in working with difficult stakeholders.

Uncover the Source of the Difficulty

The project manager must understand, as clearly as possible, the root causes for the difficult stakeholder's behavior. In some cases, this may be obvious. The difficult stakeholder may have clearly communicated the cause of concern. In other cases, however, the project manager may need to conduct research and detective work to determine the true cause of the difficulty.

Project managers might ask other people on the project team for their perspective on why the difficult stakeholder is behaving the way they are. Also, project managers can review written correspondence they have had with the difficult stakeholder and replay in their minds any conversations and interactions. In this review, they should pay particular attention to the first signs of disagreement. If a difficult stakeholder initially supported the project and now is creating problems for the project the project manager should go through a time line sequence of events to uncover the precise moment when the stakeholder shifted. This may provide valuable clues into the root causes of the stakeholder's perspective.

Stand in the Shoes of the Difficult Stakeholder

Project managers should visualize themselves in the stakeholder's position. The project manager can do this by asking himself or herself a few questions:

- If the stakeholder's argument was valid, what are the reasons that would make it valid?
- What evidence or data might the stakeholder point to that would support the stakeholder's position?
- What actions might exacerbate the stakeholder's concerns—that is, make him or her even more resistant to the project's direction?
- Is there anything that can be done to reasonably mitigate the concerns?

After thinking through each of these questions, project managers have a better understanding of what they are dealing with. Armed with this information, they should think through what, if anything, they can do to help move the difficult stakeholder in the proper direction.

Engage the Project Sponsor

Managing difficult stakeholders is an excellent opportunity to engage the executive project sponsor. Engaging the executive sponsor is helpful to the project manager in three ways.

First, it notifies the sponsor that there is a potential problem and gives the sponsor an opportunity to work with the project manager to manage the problem before it becomes larger.

Second, the sponsor may have a different perspective on the project and offer insights into the root causes. If possible, engage the executive sponsor in a conversation about the questions listed in the preceding section in regard to seeing the conflict from the stakeholder's perspective. The sponsor may have additional thoughts on the stakeholder's concerns.

Third, working with the executive sponsor provides support for the project manager. Project managers typically do not have formal position authority. Executive sponsors, however, typically do have position authority and can make things happen if necessary. When dealing with difficult stakeholders, it is helpful to the project manager to engage the support of someone with formal position authority.

Develop a Plan of Action

Each stakeholder conflict has unique attributes. A custom plan should be developed to mitigate each conflict. Working together with the executive sponsor, the project manager should develop the plan. The plan might include a wide range of options such as the following:

- Conduct a one-on-one meeting with the difficult stakeholder to find a path to agreement.
- Communicate, for the first time, select project details that may not be known by the difficult stakeholder.
- Re-communicate any project details the stakeholder may not have understood when he or she previously heard them.
- Ask the stakeholder for input on how to resolve the disagreement.
- Engage a third party with a strong relationship to both the difficult stakeholder and either the project manager, the executive sponsor, or one of the members of the Executive Council.
- Add a new stakeholder to the project who may serve as a balance to the difficult stakeholder.
- Diplomatically remove the difficult stakeholder from the project.

The project manager and the executive sponsor should use their awareness and creativity to develop the best plan of action for the situation. Difficult stakeholders should be managed directly, firmly, and diplomatically.

Execute and Monitor the Plan

After the project manager and the executive sponsor agree to a plan of action, the next step is to execute the plan. In most cases, the project manager takes the leadership role in executing the plan. Even if not personally involved in the plan of action, the project manager ensures that the appropriate actions are taken. The project manager tracks results and report back to the executive sponsor. As needed, the plan should be revised.

In some situations the executive sponsor takes the leadership role in resolving the conflict. If the executive sponsor has a relationship, for example, with the difficult stakeholder, then it may be best for the executive sponsor to personally have a discussion with the difficult stakeholder. Another scenario where the executive sponsor should take the lead is when the executive sponsor knows a third party who can mediate between the project team and the difficult stakeholder. The executive sponsor's personal relationships help smooth the way for action.

It is important to not create any more conflict than necessary. The project manager should be careful to diplomatically execute the plan when dealing with difficult stakeholders. The same difficult stakeholder may be on future projects, and the other stakeholders who are observing the conflict may be on other projects, too. They will establish opinions of the project manager in part by observing how the project manager deals with adversity.

Project managers, however, should not shy away from fighting for their cause. They must be respected if they are to get things done in their organization or across external organizations. Project managers who diplomatically defend their positions earn the respect of their project stakeholders and thereby increase their ability to take the actions necessary to achieve project success.

Delphi Technique

Developed in the 1950s, the Delphi technique is most commonly used for decisions involving forecasting and estimating. It has been used to predict technology trends, resolve public policy issues, and gain consensus around forward-looking business decisions.

The Delphi technique involves a panel of experts answering questions in a series of rounds. The technique works only if the experts have accurate knowledge about the decision. Using the Delphi technique to create decisions from a panel of uniformed or misinformed stakeholders only yield more confidence around an ignorant answer.

The expert panel is typically anonymous. Each panel member is given a survey or questionnaire. Completed surveys are returned to a facilitator. The facilitator reviews all responses, eliminates information that is irrelevant, and then compiles the remaining results into a document that is returned to the panelists. Experts then provide additional feedback on their ideas and others' ideas, including the reasoning behind their feedback. The facilitator compiles results again and continues to go through the process as many times as necessary.

Unlike the behavior demonstrated in the Delphi technique, in group meetings people may be inclined to protect their initial opinions and engage in debate with other experts. In the anonymity of the Delphi technique, however, experts may shift away from their initial comments, feel less need to engage in debate, and even correct their own errors without risk of embarrassment. Also, because they are anonymous, the experts are often open to share perspectives that may be different from those they are known for. The experts may engage in debate with others without fear or anxiety that may come from debating an influential expert or a powerful individual. When participating in group meetings, individuals may tend to conform to the group leader—a phenomenon mitigated with the Delphi technique.

Source: Kesten C. Green, J. Scott Armstrong, and Andreas Graefe, "Methods to Elicit Forecasts from Groups: Delphi and Prediction Markets Compared," *Foresight*, issue 8 (Fall 2007).

Proceeding without the Executive Sponsor

Regrettably, in some cases the project manager may be required to manage difficult stakeholders without the assistance of the executive sponsor. This situation may occur because the executive sponsor does not have the time to help the project manager. In other situations, the executive sponsor may not have the ability or interest in helping. And in still other situations, the executive sponsor may be the difficult stakeholder themselves. In each of these situations the responsibility to create the plan of action falls on the shoulders of the project manager.

This does not mean the project manager needs to manage the difficult stakeholder entirely on his or her own. If at all possible, the project manager should seek the assistance of a key executive stakeholder other than the executive sponsor in developing a plan of action. As discussed earlier, there are benefits to the project manager of aligning with an executive stakeholder. These benefits include notifying the key executive in the organization there is a problem before it gets worse, providing the executive stakeholder the opportunity to proactively solve the problem, and obtaining a different perspective from the project manager on context around the difficult stakeholder and potential courses of action. When dealing with sensitive issues, it is best to have open communication with key individuals in the organization in a position to help the project manager.

Positive Attitude

The project manager's attitude is mirrored by project stakeholders. This point cannot be overstated. A confident project manager, as discussed earlier in this book, leads to stakeholders who are more confident in a successful project. A skittish or confused project manager leads to concerned stakeholders. Everything the project manager does should be completed in a positive and effective manner.

A positive and big-picture outlook is particularly important when dealing with difficult stakeholders. Do not allow one difficult

Communicating with a Difficult Stakeholder

There is no one best technique to manage difficult stakeholders. However, there are some guidelines: be transparent, be consistent, and be persistent.

- *Be transparent.* Project managers should clearly communicate their perspective and the reasoning behind it. The message must also be understandable. Stakeholders must understand what the project manager is saying before they can react to it.
- *Be consistent.* Project managers should have a consistent message regardless of whom they are talking to. A consistent message improves the project manager's credibility and builds trust with stakeholders.
- *Be persistent.* Working with stakeholders is often a long-term proposition. The project manager should not expect immediate results. There may be delays and confusion that slow down the project.

See Chapter 12, Negotiation, for more details on reaching agreement with stakeholders.

stakeholder to derail the entire project. The project manager should put the situation with the difficult stakeholder into context and not lose focus on the goal of the project—to deliver results. It is likely that the rest of the project management team can continue doing what they're doing and moving the project in a positive direction. It is the project manager's choice to keep the project team focused on the work at hand or to focus the team's time on the difficult stakeholder. It is typically best to deploy the former strategy: keep the team focused on their work and don't let the difficult stakeholder become a distraction.

A team focused entirely on a difficult stakeholder is a team that is likely to fail. It is the project manager's responsibility, as pilot in

Landing Gear Okay—Landing Light Broken

A commercial airliner is setting up for a landing. The captain pulls the lever for the landing gear to go down. He looks at the panel for three green lights to confirm that all three sets of wheels are in the "down and locked" position. The captain sees only two lights. He taps the lights to see if there is a short circuit. No change—only two of the lights are on. The captain grows frustrated and commands the full attention of the copilot who is currently flying the airplane. The two discuss the situation and focus all of their attention on the unlit light.

The copilot, distracted by the perceived emergency, does not notice that the airplane is losing altitude. The captain, believing the copilot is still actively flying the plane, does not notice the altitude dropping either. The pilot and copilot continue to focus their full attention on the landing light situation. The plane continues to lose altitude and crashes into the ground—with all of the landing gear, three sets of wheels, down and locked. The light had burned out. There was no problem other than a burned-out light. The overreaction to the problem created a new problem that was far worse.

The moral of the story is twofold. First, don't let one difficult stakeholder create such a large distraction that the project team stops running the project. Second, most aviation accidents are a combination of bad decisions. Any good decision in the string can break the chain and avoid the accident. Great project managers would do well to recognize this when they see a series of bad decisions being made on their projects. The savvy project manager breaks the chain with a good decision to get the project back on track.

command, to model the behavior he or she wants to see from the team. This means continuing to move forward on the project and maintaining a positive attitude even in the face of adversity. This can be challenging and difficult, yet it is a trait of the most successful project managers and leaders.

See Chapter 10, Leadership, for more guidance on how to lead in a project environment.

Summary

In summary, it is not unusual for project managers to run into difficult stakeholders who do not support their project. Projects create change, and change creates challenges. The project manager's attitude in dealing with these challenges signals to the rest of the project team confidence and control . . . or frustration and even fear. The effective project manager displays confidence and control and ensures the project stays on track despite any adverse conditions that may come up.

The project manager should determine if the difficult stakeholder's support is required for the project to move forward. If the stakeholder's support is not required then the project manager can spend less time working on those issues. If the stakeholder's support is required for project success, however, the project manager must find a path to agreement.

The project manager should work diligently to understand the root cause(s) of the conflict and then see it from the perspective of the difficult stakeholder. The project manager should engage the executive sponsor, if possible, to develop a plan of action. Then the project manager should work with the executive sponsor to execute and monitor the plan of action.

It is always important for the project manager to keep in mind that difficult stakeholders come with the territory of project management. Project managers should not feel as though they're doing something wrong because there's a difficult stakeholder. Instead, it may mean they are doing something right by creating real change.

In the final section of this book we shift our focus to the general stakeholder management skills of leadership, buy-in, and negotiation. Although the next section can be applied to many life situations, it is targeted specifically at project and change management situations. Real change requires leadership, the focus of the next chapter.

Section Four

GENERAL
STAKEHOLDER
MANAGEMENT SKILLS

S ection Four provides a portfolio of general management skills the project manager can deploy in all kinds of situations. The section is divided into three chapters: Leadership, Buy-In, and Negotiation.

Chapter 10, Leadership, begins with the premise that all project managers are leaders. Project stakeholders look to the project manager to provide guidance and direction. Chapter 10 provides a situational leadership framework based on A Sixth Sense for Project Management®.

Chapter 11, Buy-In, offers a three-step process to gain support. Project stakeholders have a variety of perspectives, attitudes, and beliefs. The Buy-In chapter contains a powerful framework that is adaptable to earn the support of each project stakeholder.

Chapter 12, Negotiation, provides 10 high-impact tips the savvy project manager will deploy to succeed in project negotiations. Projects are a constant negotiation, whether about resources for the project, the time line, or the scope. In this chapter project managers learn how to get what they need for project success.

Chapter Ten

Leadership

It is better to lead from behind and to put others in front, especially when you celebrate victory when nice things occur. You take the front line when there is danger. Then people will appreciate your leadership.

Nelson Mandela

P roject managers are leaders. In this chapter we discuss the role of the project manager as leader. Specifically, we focus on the project manager's role leading stakeholders. As discussed in prior chapters of this book there are many different types of stakeholders. Therefore, there is not one leadership approach that is equally effective for all stakeholders. Successful project managers must develop and apply a variety of leadership styles. In this chapter we discuss the different leadership styles a project manager can employ and when to use each style.

Project Leaders

Managers in a Fortune 500 company meet to discuss the role of project management in their organization. Historically, the function of project management had been embedded across other responsibilities. For example, a full-time engineer might also serve as a project manager. The leadership team is discussing whether to create a separate role that is entirely dedicated to project management.

In the middle of the conversation, one of the managers says, "We do not need project managers. What we need are project leaders."

The manager's point is that the organization does not need a person focused only on milestones, tasks, and "to do" lists. What the organization needs is an individual willing and able to take responsibility for project results and delivery of outcomes.

A Sixth Sense for Project Management®

A Sixth Sense for Project Management® is a portfolio of six disciplines developed over a two-and-a-half-year process. The six disciplines create the underlying framework for the leadership model discussed in this chapter. The six disciplines are the result of input, conversation, and insights gained from a broad variety of sources.

Inputs into the six disciplines of A Sixth Sense for Project Management® include:

- Project manager surveys.
- Scientific research and related articles.
- Scientific and project management conferences.
- Extensive discussions with professional project managers.
- Consultations with various additional subject matter experts.

Information from these inputs was streamlined into the six disciplines,[1] shown in Figure 10.1.

---

[1]Tres Roeder, *A Sixth Sense for Project Management* (Bloomington, IN: Author-House, 2011).

AWARENESS
Tune Your Radar To
People and Situations

WHOLE BODY DECISIONS™
Use Your Brain, Heart and
Gut To Make Great Decisions

CLEAR COMMUNICATION
Communicate Straightforward
Thoughts, Words and Images

ADAPTABILITY
Adapt But Don't Break, Be A
Chameleon With A Core™

DIPLOMACY
Unearth Common Ground
and Influence Outcomes

PERSISTENCE
Melt Obstacles and
Visualize Success

Figure 10.1 Six Disciplines of A Sixth Sense for Project Management
Source: A Sixth Sense for Project Management®. © 2009 Roeder Consulting.

A detailed discussion of each of these disciplines can be found in the author's book *A Sixth Sense for Project Management*.

Project Managers Are Leaders

Project managers should take responsibility for organizational results. This requires leadership. Increasingly, organizations expect their project managers to understand the big-picture organizational context of their projects and guide the project team to an outcome that helps further

Table 10.1 Projects Require Leadership

Leadership Is Required When . . .	Do Projects Typically Include This Element?
People are unsure what to do.	Yes
There are different viewpoints.	Yes
A result must be delivered.	Yes
People have to work together.	Yes

the organization's goals. This journey is not a straight line. It requires project managers to develop a robust interpersonal skill set to complement their technical project management skills and business acumen. Organizations expect project managers to deliver results, and this requires more from the project manager than only tracking time lines and budgets. It requires leadership.

Project Managers Must Deliver Results

Project managers are responsible for delivering project results. The project manager's leadership, depending on the project or situation, is called upon to manage and control stakeholders, scope, budget, time lines, and the like. Others in the organization look to the project manager to provide direction. This is reasonable because the project manager is often the most knowledgeable person in regard to the projects.

Table 10.1 shows that projects require leadership. All of the situations listed in the table occur in a project environment. For example, there is uncertainty in a project environment. In uncertain times, people seek someone who can provide a path to clarity. The project manager can, and should, be the person to provide clarity to the team on how to implement the project. The executive sponsor may provide the overall vision and direction. The project manager, however, provides the day-to-day direction, motivation, and encouragement.

Most Project Managers Do Not Have Direct Authority

Research shows that most project managers do not have stakeholders directly reporting to them. Project team members are more likely to

Project Managers Must Work through Other People

Data from a series of global webinars, representing over 1,000 project managers and change leaders from more than 40 countries, show that the overwhelming majority do not have any stakeholders reporting directly to them.

Webinar participants were asked to identify all of the stakeholders in their projects—the project team, the executive sponsor, the end users of project outcomes, and so on. Then they were asked the following question: *Do any of your project stakeholders report directly to you?* The chart shows their responses.

The data in Figure 10.2 show that most project managers and change leaders do not have direct reports. Therefore, the project manager must find ways to deliver results without having the benefit of formal position authority. The project manager must work through other people.

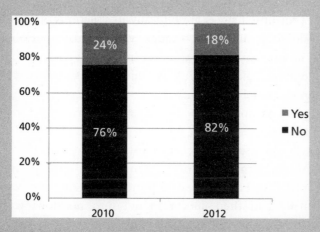

Figure 10.2 Percentage of Project Managers and Change Leaders with Direct Reports
Source: Roeder Consulting webinar polling data. © 2012 Roeder Consulting.

have a formal reporting relationship to a manager or supervisor outside of the project team. This outside manager or supervisor will control the project team member's formal performance review, job assignments, compensation adjustments, and so forth.

Project team members, however, may have an informal or dotted-line reporting relationship with the project manager. In a dotted-line reporting relationship the project manager guides the team member's activities only as related to the project. The project manager may have input into the team member's formal performance review but not the final word. This dynamic of project team members who formally report to someone other than the project manager, but are under the project manager's direction for the project, creates a unique and sometimes awkward situation that the project manager must be equipped to manage. The project manager must learn how to lead and direct the work of the team without the benefit of formal position authority.

Leading without Direct Authority

Therefore, project managers are typically in situations where they must lead without direct authority. Leaders with formal position authority may have control over annual performance reviews, compensation, work assignments, and so on. This control gives leaders with formal authority an increased probability that the direct report will follow their wishes. Formal authority does not guarantee that direct reports will follow, but it helps. The most effective leaders with formal authority, however, will still display the characteristics discussed in this section on leading without formal authority. This is encouraging for project managers as their careers progress. If project managers first learn how to lead informally and then are promoted into positions with formal position authority, they will be well prepared.

Leadership Is Dynamic

The project manager's role changes across situations. Consider the analogy of an American football team. The player holding the ball is a

Leading without Position Authority

A current course on project management leadership asks participants to identify someone who has been influential in their lives in
a positive way but who did not have direct authority over them.
The person cannot be a parent, coach, boss, or anyone else in a
position of direct authority. After participants identify this person,
they are then asked to list the person's attributes. A partial list of
their feedback follows:

- Active listener.
- Articulate.
- Takes ownership.
- Follows up.
- Careful wording.
- Honesty.
- Willingness to say, "I don't know."
- Integrity.
- Same message in different settings.
- Unselfish; more interested in others than self.
- Sense of humor.
- Compassionate.
- Competent.
- Organized.
- Respectful.
- Positive attitude.
- Does not take self too seriously.
- Open for input.
- Nonjudgmental.
- Confident.
- Has vision.
- Ability to put things in terms of the big picture.
- Intuitive.

- Knowledgeable.
- Work ethic.
- Good communicator.
- Sincere.
- Has priorities straight.
- In control of own priorities.

Classes share stories about their influential person. They discuss stories such as the adult who turns a bad-luck incident into a win, a friend who is laid off from his job and uses it as an opportunity to get into a much better and more lucrative line of work, and a child with a life-threatening disease who displays an amazing ability to lead the adults around her with a brilliantly positive attitude and pragmatic demeanor.

Project managers can develop skills around each item on the list. For example, the first item on the list is "active listener." Project managers can become active listeners. The second item on the list is "articulate." Project managers can also develop their ability to be more articulate in their communication. And so on. Each of the skills listed can be actively developed by project managers even if they do not have formal position authority. It *is* possible to be a leader without direct authority.

SOURCE: "Dynamic Leadership Skills for Better Project Results," Roeder Consulting course, part of the A Sixth Sense for Project Management® curriculum.

leader at that moment. All eyes are on that player. His decisions and actions cause others to react and follow. If he gives the ball to someone else, then the leadership also passes. All eyes are now on the new player with the ball.

Projects are similar. Some days the project manager "has the ball" on a key decision or action. Other days someone else "has the ball" and the project manager's role is to follow. Part of the art of leadership is knowing when to lead and when to follow.

Situational Leadership Model

Project managers must understand how to manage a variety of stake-holders in a variety of situations. The situational leadership model will help the project manager understand the appropriate leadership approach to use with each stakeholder. This situational leadership model follows three steps: aware, adapt, and act.

Leadership Model Step #1: Aware

Awareness, the first discipline of A Sixth Sense for Project Management®, is the foundational skill for understanding the interpersonal aspect of projects. As has been discussed in a number of chapters in this book, successful project stakeholder management requires keen aware-ness on the part of the project manager. Since there is no one approach that always works with project stakeholders awareness will help project managers understand how to tailor their approach to the situation at hand. We will discuss awareness in the following three categories:

1. Self-awareness.
2. Awareness of others.
3. Situational awareness.

Self-Awareness

Each project manager has their own unique personal style. Self-awareness helps project managers become more comfortable with their own personality traits, habits, and attitudes that form their personal style and leadership behavior. The best leaders understand their core. It is important for project team stakeholders to understand who the project manager is and what he or she stands for.

The project manager is encouraged to take a program to develop self-awareness. This program might include a personality profile; however, it should not be limited to a personality profile. Personality profiles, such as the Myers–Briggs Type Indicator (MBTI®) and the DiSC® Profile, help people learn more about their personal attributes. Many project managers find this to be helpful.

Individuals, however, should not stop exploring self-awareness after taking a personality profile because self-awareness is dynamic. Project managers are likely to have aspects of their approach and personality that change based on the situation, how rested they are, how much stress they are under, and other variables. Therefore, project managers are also encouraged to pursue ongoing self-awareness throughout their careers to learn how to read their own personal attributes in all situations.

Awareness of Others

Once the project manager is aware of self, the next step is to become more aware of others. The project manager must have knowledge of the stakeholders involved in the project.

In Section Two we discussed five groups of stakeholders: project team members, executive stakeholders, external stakeholders, stakeholders subject to the change, and phantom stakeholders. We discussed attributes of each group and techniques to understand and manage the groups. Now, we will go one level deeper and investigate differences at the individual level. Individuals in each of these groups are going to have different levels of experience and knowledge. The project manager's leadership style will vary based on these individual differences.

See Section Two, Stakeholder Groups, for more detail on project team members, executive stakeholders, external stakeholders, stakeholders subject to the change, and phantom stakeholders.

The successful project manager leverages awareness of others to better understand the variations by stakeholder. Awareness of others requires understanding verbal and nonverbal behavior. Verbal and nonverbal behavior can have different meanings across stakeholders and

Personality Profiles

Personality profiles are commonly used as self-assessment tools. These profiles can be a helpful way for project managers and their teams to learn more about themselves and others. For example, project managers might learn that they have a different personality type than one of their key stakeholders. It is helpful for both individuals to know this and learn techniques to work effectively with each other despite the differences in their styles.

Project managers are cautioned, however, against putting too much emphasis on personality profiles. It is not always possible to give a personality profile to all project stakeholders. Therefore, the project manager will typically have inadequate information about the personality styles of all of the stakeholders as measured by a personality profile. This is one reason why the project manager should not depend too heavily on the personality profile.

A second reason the project manager should not depend too heavily on personality profiles is because people are dynamic and personality profiles are static. In other words, a personality profile is taken at one point in time. The individual taking the personality profile may change over time based on any number of circumstances, such as life changes, general health, stress level, dietary changes, and how rested the person is.

Project managers must engage in awareness on an ongoing basis to assess themselves and their stakeholders. Awareness is the ongoing discipline of understanding oneself and others in the project. Only with full awareness will the project manager have the best chance of navigating the complexities of project stakeholder management.

cultures. The project manager is cautioned against making assumptions based on verbal and nonverbal behavior. Thoughtful discussions and due diligence are required to obtain an accurate and well-rounded perspective on a stakeholder's attitudes.

See Chapter 11, Buy-In, for more detail on verbal and nonverbal behavior.

Stakeholder attitudes may change over the duration of the project, so it is important to monitor stakeholder attitudes on an ongoing basis. The project manager's most reliable supporters at the beginning of a project may become resisters at the end of the project. The opposite is also true. Some people who fight the project manager diligently in the early phases of a project may become unexpected but welcome champions in the closing hours. The project manager should constantly be vigilant and aware of others.

Stakeholders in Groups

The project manager should be vigilant to observe differences in stakeholder behavior when they are meeting individually compared to meeting with a group. The project manager should not assume that a project stakeholder who supports the project in an individual meeting will also support the project in a group setting. Group dynamics are complex and can cause individuals to behave in unusual and unexpected ways. It is well known that peer pressure among teenagers can cause unwitting participants to take actions they otherwise would not take. This dynamic happens with adults, too. Group and organizational pressures can influence stakeholder perspectives.

The best way for project managers to increase their awareness of how stakeholders will react in a group setting is simply to observe them in groups. The project manager should note any differences in perspectives and viewpoints between individual meetings with the stakeholder and group meetings with the stakeholder. When observing the stakeholder's group interactions, the savvy project manager will notice who else is in the meeting. It may be noted that certain stakeholders will adjust their perspectives if specific people are in attendance.

Situational Awareness

Situational awareness refers to everything outside of self-awareness and awareness of others. Situational awareness ranges from the layout of the conference room to the latest trends in the national gross domestic product. Anything and everything that can influence the project is part of the situation.

The project manager must constantly scan the environment for new factors that might influence project outcomes. Since situational leadership addresses everything that can have an influence on the project, there is an infinitely broad range of items included in situational leadership. Project managers should keep themselves aware of situational factors by frequently asking themselves the question: "What are the forces that might impact this project?"

By routinely asking this question and assessing the probability and potential impact of the forces, project managers will grow their understanding of the situation. The project managers should develop contingency plans around how they would react to the forces that have a higher probability of occurring or that will have the most dramatic impact if they do occur. By thinking through these scenarios in advance, the project manager is more likely to have proper thinking and a calm demeanor if the situation does occur.

Leadership Model Step #2: Adapt

The second step in the leadership model, consistent with the adaptability discipline of A Sixth Sense for Project Management®, is to adapt. In the first step of the situational leadership model we focused on awareness. Awareness leads to knowledge that may require adaptation. Project managers should not be content simply being aware of what's going on around them.

Research shows that project managers who do not adapt decrease their chances of project success.[2] This is also true with leadership. If the

---

[2]Janice Thomas and Mark Mullaly, *Researching the Value of Project Management* (Newtown Square, PA: Project Management Institute, 2008).

General Colin Powell on Situational Leadership

General Colin Powell delivered a keynote address to the Project Management Institute's Global Congress in Denver, Colorado, in 2008. In his keynote address, he said that people often ask him what kind of leader he is. He said that he thought this was a silly question because he was not just one type of leader. He had many different leadership styles. He explained, for example, that he might have a person in his office one day whom he was patting on the back for a job well done. The next morning, he further explained, the same person might be in his office getting chewed out for a mistake.

General Powell adapts his leadership style to the situation and to the person. This adaptability framework, also referred to as situational leadership, doesn't work only for generals. It is an excellent foundation for project managers, too.

project manager leads all people the same way in all situations, then doing so is going to make things worse in some situations. The behavior that works for one person may be the absolute wrong way to lead another person. Also, the way to lead the *same person* in one situation may be very different from the most effective way to lead that person in a different situation. Project managers must adapt their processes and styles to what their awareness is telling them. Next, we discuss how specifically project managers should adjust their behavior.

Adapting to Time and Capability

The situational leadership model is based on two attributes: time and capability. We discuss each in more detail next.

Time   The first attribute of the situational leadership model is the amount of time available until action is required. (See Figure 10.3.) Consider a situation where time is limited. In these urgent situations

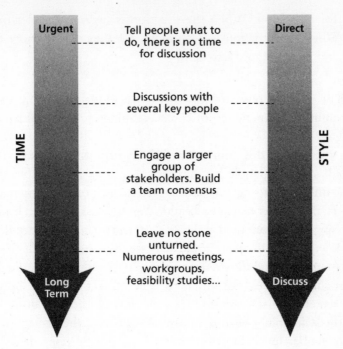

Figure 10.3 Time Continuum
© 2012 Roeder Consulting.

leaders are called upon to tell people what to do right away. There is no time for discussion or debate. Decisions must be made quickly and decisively.

As we move down the continuum the leader has more time. Let's say the situation is pressing but the project manager does not need to make a decision immediately. The project manager can now include a small group of stakeholders into the decision. As we continue to move lower on the continuum, there is more time for discussion. With more time, the project manager can address a larger audience of stakeholders. Talking to a larger group of stakeholders will help the project manager achieve broad-based support. It also enables the project manager to capture input from a more diverse group of people, increasing the probability that the action will be the best one.

Continue to the bottom of the continuum where there is plenty of time. A leader can address a very broad range of people. Studies and polls can be conducted. There is time for a deep level of due diligence. There is time for discussion. When the situation is urgent, a leader must be direct. When the situation is not urgent, a leader can be more collaborative and engaged in discussions.

Capability   The second attribute of the situational leadership model is the capability or experience of the stakeholder or stakeholder group. (See Figure 10.4.)

On the left of this continuum we begin with the inexperienced stakeholder. When people are inexperienced they generally want to be told not only *what* to do but also *how* to do it. For inexperienced stakeholders, the project manager should adapt to a task-oriented leadership style. Using a task-oriented style, the project manager is detailed and highly descriptive as to what should be done. As the stakeholder becomes more experienced and moves to the right on the continuum, the project manager should be less task-oriented. The project manager should still tell the stakeholder what should be done, but not how to do it.

As the stakeholder becomes more experienced, the project manager can give higher-level direction. Instead of specific tasks described in

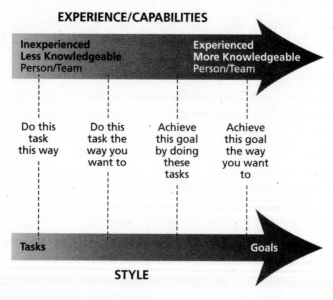

Figure 10.4   Experience Continuum
© 2009 Roeder Consulting.

detail like those given to inexperienced stakeholders, the project manager can give the stakeholder higher-level goals. All the way to the right of the continuum we find our most experienced stakeholders. Invite them into the conversation on what the goals should be.

Tasks and Goals

Using the example of a construction project, we can demonstrate the difference between tasks and goals. In this example, the project manager is responsible for overseeing the construction of a stretch of road that includes straightaways, turns, and several bridges.

If the project manager is working with a highly experienced project team member, he or she might delegate to that person the goal of overseeing construction of one of the bridges. The project manager should explain the requirements for the bridge, such as how much weight it has to bear, how long it will be, and other high-level details. The project manager then directs the project team member to the appropriate areas where the team member can find additional information. Also, the project manager notifies the individual that the project manager is always available for questions or clarifications. After delegating the goal, the project manager should monitor the project team member's performance on a regular basis and make adjustments as necessary.

A project manager who is working, however, with a less experienced team member should guide this team member with specific tasks. Instead of delegating oversight of the bridge to the team member, the project manager should provide specific action items, or tasks, with details on how to complete them. For example, the project manager might direct the team member to order the steel for the bridge. The project manager should meet with the team member and describe in detail the requirements for the steel, the date the steel must be received by, the budget for the steel, and so on. The project manager should then actively monitor the team member's actions as he or she goes through the process of procuring the steel.

Choosing the Best Leadership Style for Groups

In a group meeting project managers must decide which style(s) to use. The continuum in Figure 10.4, in addition to helping project managers determine which style to use for individual stakeholders, will also help the project manager select the best style for groups. If the project team, for example, is inexperienced, then the project manager should use the style on the left side of the continuum. If the project stakeholder team is more experienced, then the project manager should use the style on the right. Many teams have people with different experience levels. There may be some project stakeholders who have worked on projects for years and others who are new to the profession. It may be difficult in such circumstances to determine which style to use. It is best to err toward the left. If project managers are too specific in a group setting, they can be forgiven by more experienced people. However, if project managers are not specific enough, they risk project confusion and failed deliverables.

Adapting the Leadership Style

Let's use the example of a three-person group meeting to demonstrate how project managers can adapt their style in real time during a meeting of project team stakeholders.

In addition to the project manager, the project team meeting includes an inexperienced project team member (Ajay) and a very experienced team member (Natasha). The project manager wants to delegate work to each person. The conversation might go something like this:

Project Manager: Ajay, welcome to the team.
Ajay: Thank you.
Project Manager: I would like your help compiling data from a recent customer survey. As you might know, we conduct surveys on a monthly basis.
Ajay: Yes, I heard something about that.

Project Manager: Great. I will send you a spreadsheet with customer survey responses. Each question has four multiple-choice answers. I'd like you to tell me the percentage of respondents who selected each choice. We have a template you should use to compile and report this information. I will send it to you and then schedule a separate meeting to go through the process.

Ajay: That sounds good. Thank you.

Project Manager: Natasha, I saw you celebrated your 20-year anniversary with the company last week. Congratulations.

Natasha: Thank you. I really appreciate the nice celebration hosted by the Project Management Office.

Project Manager: Natasha, we're going to conduct our standard market research for this project. Can you help us out with that?

Natasha: Sure. When do you need it?

Project Manager: We need the final results in six weeks. There will be a status check three weeks from now. I'll send you a meeting invitation for the status check. As always, reach out to me if any questions come up.

Natasha: Okay. Thank you.

The project manager in this example used a task-oriented style with Ajay, the inexperienced project manager. The project manager described what needed to be done and how to do it. The project manager scheduled a separate meeting with Ajay to get into the details to be respectful of Natasha's time in today's meeting. The project manager did not want to require Natasha to sit through a detailed task-based description of information she already knew.

With Natasha, the experienced team member, the project manager provided crisp goal-oriented direction. The project manager plans to schedule a follow-up meeting in a few weeks with no other intervention before then unless asked for by Natasha or required by the situation.

Risks of Using an Incorrect Style

There is risk in using an incorrect leadership style. Look at the example of Ajay and Natasha. If the project manager had delegated goals to Ajay, the less experienced project manager, Ajay might not have known what to do. Worse, inexperienced stakeholders are often reluctant to openly share that they do not know what to do. They want and need direction but are frequently afraid to ask for it. It might be weeks or months before the problem is identified. The delay might put project time lines at risk and also diminish the quality of the work product.

Natasha, in the example, is a highly experienced stakeholder. If the project manager had incorrectly used a task-oriented style with her, giving her detailed step-by-step instructions, she might have become resentful. It would have been a waste of time for her and the project manager to go through details she already knows. It is important to understand each project stakeholder and select the best leadership style for that person and the situation.

The Leadership Matrix

Combining the two continuums (amount of time and level of experience) into a single two-by-two matrix results in a comprehensive chart that can be used by the project manager to select the best leadership style. (See Figure 10.5.)

The vertical axis of this matrix is time. Even though the simplifying two-by-two matrix divides time into only two sections, urgent and

	LOW EXPERIENCE	HIGH EXPERIENCE
URGENT	Direct Tasks	Direct Goals
LONG TERM	Discuss Tasks	Discuss Goals

Figure 10.5 2×2 Leadership Matrix of Both Continuums
© 2009 Roeder Consulting.

long-term, it is important to understand it is still a continuum. Project situations can fall anywhere along the vertical axis.

The horizontal axis is the experience level. The experience continuum, similar to the time continuum, has been divided into two sections, low experience and high experience. Although the chart only shows two sections, a stakeholder can be anywhere along the continuum.

In each cell in the matrix the appropriate leadership style is shown. For example, in the top left cell the project manager is working with an inexperienced stakeholder in an urgent situation. Urgent situations call for a direct leadership style. Inexperienced stakeholders are best managed with a task-oriented style, or simply tasks. Combining the two together we have "direct tasks."

Moving clockwise across the figure the next cell represents stakeholders with experience in an urgent situation. The project manager still must use a direct style because the situation is urgent. However, instead of a task-oriented approach the project manager and the stakeholder are better served by goals. The result is "direct goals."

The cell in the bottom right represents experienced stakeholders in situations where there is more time. The project manager should still use goals instead of tasks because the stakeholder is experienced. Since there is more time, however, the project manager can shift from a direct style to one that is more consensus-based and includes discussion. Putting this together we have "discuss goals."

Finally, the bottom left corner describes stakeholder management situations where there is time and the stakeholder is inexperienced. The project manager should deploy a task-oriented style because the inexperienced stakeholder will require very specific direction. However, because there is more time, instead of using the direct style the project manager can spend more time training the inexperienced stakeholder with discussion. Putting this together we have "discuss tasks."

Adapting Leadership Styles—Fire Captain Example

The fire captain arrives at the scene of a house fire. It is late at night. The dark sky is alight with flames leaping three stories into the air. Fortunately, everyone is already safely out of the house.

The neighbors are out of their houses, too. Flames shooting horizontally out of the second-floor windows are dangerously close to the neighbors' houses. The captain must act fast.

The situation is urgent on the time continuum, so it calls for the captain to be direct. There is no time for discussion. The captain calls Eva, the most senior firefighter.

"Lead out to the front," she tells Eva. Eva knows from experience that leading out to the front means to get a line[3] and start putting out the fire in front of the house. The captain has directed Eva with a goal. This is the "direct goals" leadership style. The captain does not tell her how to do it because she already knows.

Next, the captain calls Antonio, who just graduated from firefighter school. His badge is shiny and without scratches, dents, or smoke damage.

"Antonio, I want you drop a line and cover the exposure. Take Rob here and go to the engine. Grab a line and pull it to that point in the front yard," the captain says as she points to a spot that is close to one neighbor's house. "Then, give the signal to activate the line and start spraying the neighbor's house and any other property on that side that is in danger of catching fire. Got it?"

"Yes," Antonio nods as he grabs Rob by the arm and runs to the engine.

The captain just deployed the "direct task" leadership style with Antonio. Even if Antonio has been trained to do everything the captain just told him, it is not known what will happen when he is confronted with the real-world pressure of a live situation for the first time. The captain told him everything he needed to know to get the job done and will be watchful of him.

This story illustrates the importance of determining which leadership style to use with *a specific person in a specific situation*. The next day, the fire captain may encounter a different situation and select a different leadership style (see the next example).

---

[3]A fire hose is called a line by firefighters.

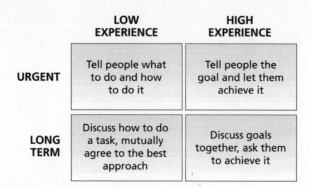

Figure 10.6   Detailed 2×2 Leadership Matrix
© 2009 Roeder Consulting.

Using a few key words from each of the four leadership styles, we can re-create the leadership matrix with a simple phrase to describe each of the four leadership styles. (See Figure 10.6.)

In Figure 10.6 "direct tasks" has been further described as "tell people what to do and how to do it." The situation is urgent, so the project manager must provide direction and "tell people what to do." In the top left quadrant we are working with an inexperienced stakeholder, so the project manager should also tell the stakeholder "how to do" the specific task or assignment.

Moving to the top right quadrant, the project manager is not required to outline how to do it because the experienced stakeholders already know how. The situation is still urgent, so the project manager should describe what must happen. In other words, the project manager must "tell people the goal and let them achieve it."

In the bottom right quadrant, a project manager working with experienced stakeholders should deploy a style that is more conversational than directive. The project manager should respect the stakeholders' experience and not talk down to them. The project manager still has deliverables, of course, so in addition to sharing the goal with the experienced stakeholders the project manager should also make it clear that they are expected to achieve the goal. The project manager will "discuss the goal together and ask people to achieve it."

Finally, in the bottom left quadrant a learning opportunity is created for the inexperienced stakeholder. The savvy project manager will use the time they have to help make the discussion with the stakeholder a learning opportunity. These types of discussions will accelerate the inexperienced stakeholder's journey to the right side of the matrix as an experienced stakeholder. The project manager might also invite the stakeholder to offer his or her own thoughts on how to achieve the task. With the project manager's guidance, the proper path will be planned. Putting it all together, the project manager will "discuss how to do a task and mutually agree to the best approach."

The Leadership Model Is Dynamic

The leadership model simplifies decisions for the project manager. After learning the model, the project manager can quickly glance at one of the matrices to determine how to lead a particular stakeholder. Each time the project manager enters a new situation he or she should reassess the team and their capabilities relative to the task at hand. As highlighted in the example, a person who is experienced in one situation may be a novice in other situations, and vice versa.

In addition to paying attention to the primary attributes in the leadership model, time and experience, there are other aspects of stakeholders that will cause project managers to change their leadership style. Several items might lead project managers to rethink the style they plan to use with a stakeholder.

Stakeholder attributes that may cause the project manager to use a different leadership style include:

- Anxiety.
- Doubt or lack of self-confidence.
- Sleep deprivation.
- Emotional stress.

In general, these characteristics will move stakeholders to the left in the model. In other words, an experienced stakeholder who is suffering from sleep deprivation may require a more task-oriented and hands-on

Situations May Change the Relative Experience Level of Stakeholders

Two days after the house fire, the fire crew is called to the scene of a medical emergency. The captain sits in the engine as it screams toward the scene of the accident. She reflects on the house fire two days before. She is proud of her team. They contained the fire and saved the neighbors' houses. The captain's fast thinking and adaptive leadership style delivered results. Quickly, her thoughts turn to the new situation. Most of her team has not been trained on medical emergencies. In fact, the only person on her team who is a medic is the rookie, Antonio. It is going to be another urgent situation. Even though he's new to the squad, Antonio is the most experienced person in this situation.

The driver of the fire engine pulls down a narrow road in a residential neighborhood and stops in front of a home. There is a person lying on the ground who appears to have fallen from a ladder. It looks like the victim has a broken leg. The captain jumps off the engine.

"Antonio," she says to the brand-new firefighter, "you're our medic. Get to work. Eva, help him."

"Got it, Chief," Antonio replies. "Eva, get oxygen and a first aid kit from the engine and catch up with me," he says as he takes off in the direction of the victim.

The captain has just used the "direct goals" leadership approach with the rookie. She selected this option because in this situation Antonio has the most experience of anyone on the team—he is the only medic on the squad. Further, the captain herself has not been trained as a medic, so it would not be possible for her to direct tasks. She has not been trained on what to do. Any leader using direct tasks must know what he or she is doing. With this new situation, Antonio has shifted from being the least experienced firefighter to being the most experienced.

Further, Antonio used a "direct tasks" leadership style with Eva, the most senior firefighter. Antonio knows Eva is not a trained medic so she will need specific direction on what to do.

leadership style. Ability often decreases in sleep-deprived individuals, so the project manager should more closely monitor the work of stakeholders who have not had proper rest. This is particularly important if the project team stakeholder's work is on the critical path.

Adapting Leadership Style to Temporary Personal Circumstances

It seems like a regular day on the job for the fire captain. She's back in the engine heading to a house fire. She reflects on her team and their abilities on that day. As she thinks about her team, though, she quickly realizes something is different today. Eva, a 20-year veteran, does not seem to be herself. The captain does not know all the details, but Eva did mention she is going through a challenging move to a new home. There are some leaks in the new house' plumbing and some difficult discussions with the prior owner. When the captain did roll call that morning, she could tell Eva was not herself. Eva mentioned something about discussions she is having with an attorney and all of the paperwork, stress, and hassles of filing a complaint against the former owner. Life's problems usually did not get to Eva, but today seemed different.

The fire engine comes to an abrupt halt and brings the captain back to the current moment. She looks out of the fire engine and sees a fire that is quickly growing. Making a quick decision in this urgent situation, the captain decides to adapt to a more task-oriented style with Eva. Eva will be her second up, meaning the captain and Eva will stay together while the others will immediately begin to work on putting out the fire. She certainly does not want to offend Eva but also feels it is her responsibility as the team leader to protect Eva's safety and the team's safety, and also to ensure the effectiveness of the team's overall mission. Also, everyone takes a turn at being second up, so Eva might not even know that the captain has adapted her leadership style out of concern.

Leadership Model Step #3: Act

The third step in the leadership model is to take action. Actions should not be taken until the project manager has made himself or herself aware of the situation and adapted the leadership style accordingly. Even in urgent situations the project manager should take a few moments to assess the situation before acting.

Project leadership is a skill built on the shoulders of all six disciplines of A Sixth Sense for Project Management®. The first two steps of the leadership model are aware and adapt, which align directly with Awareness and Adaptability, two of the disciplines of A Sixth Sense for Project Management®. The third step of the leadership model, act, is composed of the remaining four disciplines of A Sixth Sense for Project Management®: Whole Body Decisions™, Clear Communication, Diplomacy, and Persistence. Next, we discuss how these remaining disciplines relate to taking actions and becoming a better project leader.

Whole Body Decisions™

Leaders make decisions. Great leaders make great decisions. The best way to make great decisions is to follow the process of Whole Body Decisions™. Whole Body Decisions™ are made with a combination of the brain, the heart, and the gut.

Project managers may observe many different approaches to decision making in their project environment. A few examples are:

- Avoidance—ignore there's a decision to make.
- Uninformed—flip a coin.
- Analytical—the quantitative facts and just the facts.
- Gut feeling/intuition—make the decision by "feel."

None of these approaches are optimal on their own. Whole Body Decisions™ involve all available information sources (that is, the brain, heart, and gut) and therefore have the highest probability of yielding the best decisions. Making no decision is still a decision. If project managers do nothing they have *decided* to do nothing. In the words of General Patton, "Be prepared to make decisions. That's the most important quality in a good leader."

A Whole Body Decision

A project manager is confronted with an urgent situation. One of the key project vendors just sent notification that it will miss the deadline. The contract shows a clear delivery date and also states that the project manager can cancel the contract if the delivery date will not be met. The project manager has the option, therefore, of sticking with the current delinquent vendor or starting from the beginning with a new vendor. A decision must be made today. Lionel, the team member responsible for the vendor contract, is inexperienced. The project manager decides to use the "direct tasks" leadership style with Lionel. The project manager selects direct tasks because the situation is urgent and Lionel is inexperienced.

The project manager learned about Whole Body Decisions™ in a training program and feels this approach should be used. The project manager starts with the information in his brain. What are the analytical details? How much time will it take for a new vendor to get up to speed? Is the current vendor likely to have further delays? What are the cost implications?

Many of these facts are unknown. The project manager closes his eyes and tunes in to his heart and his gut. The project manager thinks about continuing the current relationship. His gut tightens and his heart rate picks up. He thinks about all of the problems they've already had. Then the project manager thinks about what it would be like to work with a different vendor. There is a different vendor he's had a few conversations with that seems to be organized and competent. He feels a sense of calm. His heart rate slows down.

He can't put his finger on it, but he gets a feeling that his best option is to secure a new vendor. He opens his eyes and goes back to the data on his desk. He double-checks costs and time lines. Yes, he decides, the team can make this work. In fact, he says to himself, it will work even better than staying with the current vendor. He decides to switch vendors and will direct Lionel to make the change. Also, he will explain to Lionel how to initiate the paperwork for a new vendor. The project manager has led with direct tasks and has successfully deployed the proper technique for Whole Body Decisions™ to inform the project team's direction.

Clear Communication

Let's say the project manager has demonstrated acute awareness and made highly effective Whole Body Decisions™. The project manager, however, has not been able to effectively communicate these decisions to the project stakeholders. The project does not react to the decisions. In this situation the project manager's awareness and decision making are wasted. The project is unchanged.

Decisions do not have impact unless they are appropriately and effectively communicated. All relevant stakeholders should know what has been decided. The project manager should also communicate the rationale behind the decisions. Stakeholders want to understand what has been decided and why.

Leadership is intertwined with the ability to communicate. Stakeholders cannot be led by the project manager if they do not understand what the project manager wants. Communication is the vehicle the project manager uses to help execute actions. Projects require action. Successful team action requires each member of the team to be pushing in the same direction. Clear communication enables this unified action by helping team members understand which way to go.

The project manager should use multiple communication channels to be most effective. In-person meetings, virtual meetings, phone calls, written communication, and the like can be deployed. Also, highly effective communicators will use stories, imagery, and analogies to get their points across. People are more likely to recall stories, and analogies are an effective way to help people understand new or complex concepts.

See Chapter 7, Stakeholder Communication, for more guidance on how to clearly communicate.

Getting the Point Across with Analogies

Analogies point out the similarity between two things and are often used to explain or clarify. Analogies are an effective tool to help stakeholders understand new ideas or concepts.

New ideas can be difficult for stakeholders to understand. The project manager can aid stakeholder understanding by connecting the new idea to a familiar idea through the use of analogies. Neurologically, this helps the stakeholder "connect the dots" in the person's brain.

For example, compare the following two descriptions:

Scenario One: The project manager explains a concept using technical project management terms.

Project Manager: We have a firm deliverable date on this project. There are various interdependencies in this project connected by finish-to-start milestones. The critical path must be followed. Our earned value is lagging.
Stakeholder: Earned what?

Scenario Two: The project manager explains a concept through the use of an analogy.

Project Manager: This project is like a relay race. If we don't get the baton into the next runner's hand by June 5th they can't proceed.
Stakeholder: I understand. We can't miss the due date and still expect to win. Please let me know how I can help.

The stakeholder clearly understands the project manager's description in scenario two. It is common knowledge that each runner in a relay race needs the prior runner to reach them before they can begin. Comparing the project to a relay race is more easily understood than project management jargon such as "we have various interdependencies in this project connected by finish-to-start milestones." The analogy helps the stakeholder understand the importance of meeting the project deadline. The project can't be delayed and the stakeholder is prepared to help.

Project managers' actions must be consistent with the directions they are communicating. One of the top forms of communication is leadership by example. We've all heard the saying that "actions speak louder than words." So, if project managers want everyone to show up to meetings on time, they must be there on time or even early. If project managers want others to work extra hours, then they should work extra hours too. When team members see the project manager modeling these behaviors, they are more likely to follow.

Diplomacy

Diplomacy is the ability to lead stakeholders in a positive and inclusive manner. Diplomacy is particularly important for project managers because most project managers must lead without direct authority. There are three characteristics of diplomatic leadership:

1. Treat people with respect.
2. Make consistent decisions.
3. Solicit feedback to continually understand the diplomatic landscape.

Treat People with Respect   Stakeholders react not only to the content of the messages coming from the project team but also to *how* the messages are communicated. Stakeholders will judge the tone of the project communications. Stakeholders may ask themselves the following questions:

- Is this the complete story or is it biased?
- Did the project team listen to my concerns?
- Is the project team open to feedback?
- Are the project team leaders leveling with me and not talking down to me in this communication?

Stakeholders are more likely to follow the project team's direction if they feel they've been treated with respect. When project managers treat people with respect and genuine concern, they are creating an environment in which people want to follow them. True leadership is creating an environment where people want to follow. The question the project manager should ask is: "Why would anyone want to follow me?"

Authenticity is one reason why stakeholders will follow. The project manager should strive to be genuine, authentic, and honest. These attributes in the project manager will give stakeholders more confidence in the project manager's actions.

Make Consistent Decisions   Stakeholders judge leaders, in part, by the consistency of their decisions. People want to follow leaders who they believe apply decisions consistently and justly. Even if the leader is making difficult decisions the organization is more likely to be supportive if members believe there is a shared burden in overcoming the difficulty.

Consistent Decision Making

A Fortune 500 company is conducting an organizational realignment. In this realignment some people are required to relocate geographically. The project team develops a common set of criteria that will be used to determine who must relocate. The project team understands that it is important for them to consistently apply these criteria to all individuals.

One of the individual project stakeholders subject to the change asks for an exception to the decision criteria. An exception is granted. This exception is viewed by other individual project stakeholders subject to the change in a negative way. They argue that all stakeholders should have been treated consistently.

In this situation it would have been wise for management to stick to the decision criteria. The problem arose with select stakeholders not because of the decision criteria, but because the decision criteria were not consistently applied and the reason for the exception was not explained.

There are times when there should be exceptions to the rule. However, management must be very careful when making exceptions and must explain to others why the exception has been made.

It is important to note, however, that the project manager can still make exceptions in extenuating circumstances. Most people understand that sometimes there need to be exceptions to the rules. When exceptions are made, however, the project manager must be honest and open about why the exception was made. The project manager should help people understand the rationale for the decision so they can see for themselves that it was reasonable.

Solicit Feedback   Effective leaders constantly scan the environment to make sure they are knowledgeable about what is going on. In the project environment, the savvy project manager will keep close tabs on how the project team is performing against the project deliverables. Awareness will help the project manager do this. The effective project manager talks to people and asks them for feedback. Do not wait for people to complain after a problem has already expanded to unacceptable levels.

Identify items that may be figuratively beneath the radar. Very low-flying airplanes and other objects can escape detection by radar by hugging the contours of the ground. This concept applies to projects, too. There are things happening that may be very important but beneath the radar of the formal project metrics and reports. Effective project managers stay in close contact with the stakeholders who are closest to the action. Through awareness and relationships they fill in the gaps where their radar—that is, their metrics and reports—are not sufficient.

It is important to note that a project manager who asks for feedback must be prepared to act on it. A project manager asking for feedback and then ignoring it is far better off never asking for the advice in the first place.

People are more likely to view projects in a positive light if they are actively asked for their input. Soliciting input is one of the key elements of earning buy-in, as discussed in the next chapter.

See Chapter 11, Buy-In, for more details on including stakeholders in the project and soliciting their feedback.

Persistence

Leaders are persistent in the pursuit of their goals. Sometimes that requires taking a step back and waiting for the right opportunity. A cat stalking a mouse waits for just the right moment to strike. A premature strike will alert the mouse to its presence. A strike that is too late will miss the opportunity.

Persistence is the last topic discussed in our leadership model for a reason. It is possible to be persistently wrong. Therefore, the project manager should be thoughtful in deciding when persistence is used. Project managers must first be aware, then adapt, and then, if they have reasonable assurance they are taking the best actions, be persistent in pursuing project success. If the actions taken do not yield the desired results, then try again. If the actions consistently fail, try different actions. Projects are not a straight line. Persistent project managers understand this and figure out ways to achieve project success.

Summary

Project managers are leaders. We discussed a three-part framework to achieve effective project leadership: aware, adapt, and act. The leadership framework is based on the fundamentals of A Sixth Sense for Project Management®. There is no one best way to lead. Effective leaders have a portfolio of leadership styles and are proficient at selecting the best style for each individual and each situation. We discussed four styles:

1. Direct tasks.
2. Direct goals.
3. Discuss tasks.
4. Discuss goals.

The project manager may often switch styles from one meeting to the next, or possibly within a meeting or conversation. As the project manager becomes more familiar with the styles it will become easier to switch quickly.

Leaders need support for their ideas. In a project environment the project manager is regularly selling the value of the project. The project manager sells the project to stakeholders to ensure its continued success. In many organizations today project managers are fighting for limited human and financial resources. Gaining support for the project is critical to obtaining and maintaining the appropriate resource level. We will discuss how to earn support for projects in the next chapter on buy-in.

Chapter Eleven

Buy-In

Speech is power: speech is to persuade, to convert, to compel.
It is to bring another out of his bad sense into your good sense.

Ralph Waldo Emerson

Project managers are routinely required to gain support for their ideas. Whether it's selling project objectives to a skeptical stakeholder, encouraging a human resources executive to provide more people for the project team, or convincing a vendor to support a change in scope, projects are one opportunity after another to earn support.

Earning support is an ongoing process, not an event. Seeking support in a single meeting or presentation is risky. Instead of using an all-or-nothing approach, it is better to design an ongoing process that earns and sustains support from stakeholders. There may be times when the only opportunity to earn support is a single meeting or presentation. However, whenever possible the project manager should think about earning support as an ongoing process.

The process starts with including people in the project. People support what they create. The second step is to observe how people are reacting. Finally, in the third step, the project manager responds based on what is observed. This three-step process is called the "Circle of Support" and is the topic of this chapter. (See Figure 11.1.)

Like any technique related to stakeholder management, the Circle of Support does not guarantee success. It does, however, increase the probability of success. Each completed step of the process brings the project manager one step closer to support.

Buy-In Is *Not* an Event

A consulting team is working on a strategy project for a Fortune 500 company. The team prepares its strategy in isolation. For weeks, the consulting team works internally to analyze, refine, and finalize its strategic recommendations. The client is rarely contacted, and most of the recommendations are not previewed with any of the client's key stakeholders before the decision meeting with executive stakeholders.

On the day of the executive meeting, the consultants present their findings. They have worked hard on their recommendations and believe they represent the best path forward for the client. The executives view and consider the findings for the first time. The consultants expect approval and next steps.

Instead, the executives ask if certain people have been included in the process. The executives want to know if their marketing executive has seen the consulting team's marketing recommendations, if the client's incentives executive has seen and reviewed the consulting team's incentive recommendations, and so on. The consultants reply that they had not included these people—their work had been mainly internal.

The consultants are sent back to talk with key people. This is an example of a failed approach to buy-in. Key stakeholders, the executives in this example, should be included before important meetings.

The Circle of Support Overview

Earning buy-in is a process, not an event. The process for earning buy-in is the Circle of Support. The Circle of Support is tailored to the role of a project manager. Most project managers do not have direct reports. Therefore, most project managers are not able to deploy a command-and-control style of earning buy-in. In other words, since most stakeholders do not report to the project manager, the project manager will have limited success directing the team from a position of power or authority. Instead, the project manager must deploy a style of buy-in that is collaborative and that helps stakeholders find the best answer for themselves.

The Circle of Support methodology is a dynamic and interactive model for the integration of new ideas into an existing organizational structure. The Circle of Support incorporates three steps:

1. Include stakeholders.
2. Observe stakeholders.
3. Respond to stakeholders.

Each step is discussed in more detail in the following subsections.

Include Stakeholders

The first step in the three-step Circle of Support process is to include stakeholders in the development and implementation of ideas. This subsection discusses the benefits of including stakeholders, who to include, and how to include them.

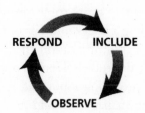

Figure 11.1 Circle of Support Graphic
© 2009 Roeder Consulting.

Benefits of Including Stakeholders

Including stakeholders in the project has two primary benefits:

1. Including people gives them personal ownership over ideas and thereby increases their support.
2. Ideas prepared together are likely to be more robust than ideas prepared in isolation.

Personal Ownership   People tend to like their own ideas. Including stakeholders in the project gives them the opportunity to inject their ideas into the project by potentially shaping the project's direction, refining how the project is implemented, or providing input into any number of other project-related decisions. Stakeholders who are included in such a manner are more likely to support the project because they have had the opportunity to provide direct input into it.

It is important, however, to clarify for stakeholders the specific areas where their input is welcome and the areas where decisions have already been made. Stakeholders typically want to know how to add value to the project, and this clarification will help them focus their efforts on the areas most valued by the project team. It is also in the project team's best interest to constructively direct the talents of their stakeholders.

Robust Ideas   Including more project stakeholders increases the volume of project feedback. This provides the project manager access to the unique perspectives, cultural backgrounds, experiences, and other assets intrinsic in each stakeholder.

Through these differences more robust project solutions are developed. One risk of including a larger number of people, however, is that it increases the number of communication channels and can increase the complexity of managing the stakeholders. To avoid an overwhelming number of stakeholders providing input and feedback on each area of the project, the project manager should be strategic in how each stakeholder is deployed.

Strategically Deploying Stakeholders

The project manager should determine the best fit in the project for each stakeholder. Finding fit includes understanding the following about each stakeholder:

- What is the stakeholder's area of expertise?
- Has the stakeholder worked on similar teams in the past?
- Where does the stakeholder live and work geographically?
- Does the stakeholder have relationships with other key stakeholders that can help with buy-in?
- How much time does the stakeholder have to devote to the project?
- Does the stakeholder prefer collaboration or individual effort?

These criteria help the project manager determine how frequently to engage the stakeholder and which specific project issues and concerns to engage the stakeholder on. Based on the responses to these questions, and others the project manager chooses to add, the project manager can find the best fit in the project for each stakeholder. Some stakeholders are team members. Others are included only in select meetings at the project manager's discretion.

Who to Include

The project manager should include individuals from a variety of backgrounds, areas of expertise, and applied experiences. Project managers are encouraged to use their awareness and knowledge of the project environment to ensure that a broad and comprehensive group of individuals are invited to be project stakeholders and included in the project.

See Section Two, Stakeholder Groups, for more information on groups of stakeholders.

Individuals to include in the project include the following:

- *Decision makers.* The project manager should identify the key decisions that must be made in the project and then investigate organizational dynamics and culture to determine who is likely to make these decisions. Sometimes decision makers are the individuals at the top of the organizational chart. In other cases, decisions are made by people at lower levels of the organization.
- *Subject matter experts.* Individuals with a high level of knowledge in one or more areas relevant to the project are subject matter experts (SMEs).
- *Thought leaders.* Every organization has people who are considered influential. These thought leaders guide organizational thinking. Sometimes the guidance from these thought leaders is obvious. For example, they may state an expert opinion in a meeting. In other

When the Project Manager Can't Pick the Project Team

Many project managers are not able to select their project team. Executive stakeholders, a Project Management Office, or some other individual or group of individuals may hand the project manager a document with the project's scope and the project's human resources who have already been assigned to the team. This does not mean, however, the project manager has no control over which stakeholders to include. Remember, the project team stakeholders (the people assigned to work on the project team) are only one of the many stakeholder groups.

Even when project managers are given a team they are not typically prevented from including others on their stakeholder list. The successful project manager engages a much larger audience than the project team. The project manager should scan the project environment to identify all stakeholders. Once they are identified, the project manager can deploy the techniques discussed in this book to include these stakeholders in the project.

cases the thought leaders may quietly and subtly advance their positions through one-on-one meetings or informal conversations. With some research, thought leaders can be found at any level of the organizational hierarchy.

- *Individuals with institutional knowledge.* If the organization has been in existence for many years it is typical to find people who have been part of the organization for a long time. These people have personally experienced different ideas, concepts, and fads. Their institutional knowledge can be beneficial to the team by helping it avoid known traps or barriers. However, the project manager should be careful not to let those with institutional knowledge block projects by saying, "We tried this before. It will never work." Project success requires an open mind and a willingness to take calculated risks.

How to Include

After all relevant stakeholders are identified the next step is to determine the best way to include them in the project. There are many different techniques the project manager and the project team can deploy to include project stakeholders. A few are listed here:

- *Interview.* Interviews can take place before, during, or after formal support is requested. Asking people's opinions is a good way to build support. Most stakeholders view this as a positive opportunity to shape ideas that guide the organization's future.
- *Update.* Stakeholder updates can be written, verbal, or in person. Updates are a tool to keep people engaged about new ideas, to share project status, and to solicit feedback.
- *Delegate.* Assign people portions of the project and make them accountable.
- *Pre-present.* Prior to large group meetings, schedule individual meetings to share key ideas and solicit feedback.

Be creative in finding ways to include stakeholders. The more customized the approach, the more likely it is to serve the specific needs of each stakeholder and the project team. Be careful, however, not to create a web of stakeholder engagement that becomes too difficult to

Engagement Groups

Creating engagement groups is a technique that helps the project manager balance the various needs of each type of stakeholder with the time constraints required to manage multiple stakeholder relationships. Engagement groups are classifications of stakeholders. For example, a project manager might place the majority of project stakeholders into one of the following groups:

- Project team members.
- Executives.
- Stakeholders Subject to the change.
- External stakeholders.

After determining the groups, the project manager sets the engagement criteria for each group across the following attributes:

- How often should the project manager communicate with each group?
- What level of detail is included in the communication?
- Will the group be allowed to influence project scope? If so, in which areas?
- Which of the tactics for including stakeholders should be deployed for each group? For example, are interviews used prior to major meetings with the group?

Using this approach, the project manager simplifies variable relationships with a large number of stakeholders into a standard approach for groups of stakeholders. This enables the project manager to create targeted customization for each group without having too many different stakeholder relationships to manage.

See Section Two, Stakeholder Groups, for more information on how to group stakeholders. Also, see Chapter 7, Stakeholder Communication, for more detail on how to communicate with the groups.

manage. The savvy project manager balances creative approaches to stakeholder engagement with pragmatic time constraints on managing all of the various stakeholder relationships. One technique the project manager is encouraged to deploy with larger groups of stakeholders is the use of engagement groups. See the inset for more detail.

Observe Stakeholders

The second step in the Circle of Support process is to observe the stakeholders. In this critical step the project manager seeks to understand each stakeholder's level of support for project objectives. Observing or tuning in to a stakeholder takes conscious effort and time. The project manager is not able to deploy the same amount of time to all stakeholders. The project manager should commit the majority of effort to those stakeholders most critical to project support. Observing includes sensitivity to both *nonverbal* and *verbal* communication.

See Chapter 3, Prioritizing Stakeholders, for guidance on how to allocate time across different stakeholders.

Nonverbal Communication

Nonverbal cues include facial expression, body positioning, and body movement (for example, whether the person is sitting still, exhibiting moderate motion, or nervously pacing the room). Nonverbal cues are not consistent across people. Crossed arms could indicate resistance in one person, or in others that they simply need a place to rest their arms. It's important to understand each individual's nonverbal habits and what they mean. There are serious risks in reading too much into people's nonverbal behavior without proper context.

Vocal cues are included in nonverbal communication. Vocal cues include tone of voice, speed of voice, and volume. In a virtual team, vocal cues are a powerful way to observe nonverbal behavior.

Nonverbal cues are often a better indicator of thoughts than verbal cues. In part, this is because it is more difficult to control how we move our hands, arms, and face (nonverbal) than it is to control what we say (verbal).

Verbal Communication

Verbal communication is the words that are used. Note that tone of voice, speed of voice, and the like are included in vocal cues, which is a subset of nonverbal behavior. Words must be carefully chosen to communicate the sender's point. Also, words must be carefully selected to be appropriate to the situation and the cultural grounding of the receiver. The project manager should select words with overall sensitivity to the reactions others may have to the words.

Respond to Stakeholders

The third step in the Circle of Support process is to respond based on what is observed. It is important to point out that this is the *third* step for intentional reasons. It is not advisable to jump to responses before including stakeholders and properly diagnosing (observing) the nature of their attitudes.

People generally display one of the three attitudes shown in Figure 11.2 or some combination thereof (e.g., someone might be unsure but leaning toward resist).

The project manager's response varies depending on where the stakeholder is on the continuum of support. Also, responses vary within each spot on the continuum. For example, as discussed later in this chapter, a rational resister is handled very differently from an emotional resister.

Support

Stakeholders in agreement with the project's objectives and tactics are supporters. The project manager's goal is to earn support from as

Figure 11.2   Resist/Unsure/Support Continuum
© 2009 Roeder Consulting.

many stakeholders as possible. After support is gained, the project manager should keep the stakeholder on the Circle of Support. People can and often do change their minds. In order to ensure ongoing support, continue to include supporters in the process. Continue to observe their attitudes and respond if it appears their support is slipping. In other words, keep the Circle of Support process going even for those who are supporters. Project support is dynamic and requires ongoing maintenance.

Unsure

Stakeholders who are unsure neither support nor resist the project. Stakeholders can be in the unsure category for one of two reasons: (1) they do not understand the project, or (2) they understand the project but are unable or unwilling to make a decision on their level of support. If someone is unsure, it is critical to determine which of these two categories the person falls into.

Do Not Understand A stakeholder who does not understand the project goals should not be considered a supporter or a resister. The project manager's first goal is to help the stakeholder understand the project. Then, the project manager can assess the stakeholder's level of support. Listed here are a few tips the project manager can deploy to help stakeholders understand the project.

- *Change the communications channel(s) in use.* People learn differently. For example, some learn from visual images, others from sound, and others from reading.
- *Map the key project ideas to something familiar.* Our brains are better able to accept new ideas if they are related to familiar ideas. Analogies and examples are great techniques to do this.
- *Have individual meetings.* Stakeholders who do not understand the project may not be comfortable asking questions or showing their lack of knowledge in a group setting. Project managers sensing that a stakeholder might not comprehend the project should consider asking the person for an individual meeting to discuss the project.

See Chapter 7, Stakeholder Communication, for more details on how to help stakeholders understand the project.

Understand but Undecided   A second group of unsure stakeholders are those who understand exactly what the project is about yet have not stated a position in support of the project or against the project. Project managers should approach these stakeholders using the techniques discussed in the following section on resisters. The key is to determine what is most important to the person. Some people may need more data or empirical evidence before lending their support. Others may have a difficult time digesting the changes and simply need emotional support. A third group may be most concerned about how the new idea impacts their standing in the organization. Proper diagnosis is the best way to ensure a proper response.

Resist

Despite the project manager's best efforts, some people resist the project. Resisters should initially be viewed positively. Their resistance may come from a reasonable disagreement about project scope and tactics. Further, resistant stakeholders may be correct in their perspective and it may be the project team that is in error. Therefore, resisters should be treated with respect and given a full opportunity to make the case for their perspective.

When resistance occurs, the project manager's first responsibility is to understand as specifically as possible where there is disagreement and why. Meet with the resisters, in person if possible, and observe very carefully what they say and how they say it. Resistance may turn into support simply by having a frank discussion. People typically respond positively when given the opportunity to discuss their perspective. Also, it may become clear that the resistance is based on a simple misunderstanding.

In this section on overcoming resistance, we discuss four tested techniques to deploy when resistance is met:

1. Ask the five why's.
2. Identify rational/emotional/political resistance.
3. Do not push so hard.
4. Negotiate.

These techniques should be deployed in the order they appear in this chapter. It is important, for example, to understand the five why's

Asking a Resister the Five Why's

Before responding, the project manager must understand why a stakeholder is resisting. The following conversation is illustrative of how a project manager can identify the true cause of resistance. This example depicts a project manager talking with the vice president of sales about a project focused on upgrading the system used for sales transactions.

Project Manager: Hello, I'd like to discuss the project with you.
Resister (vice president of sales): Sure.
Project Manager: To start, can you share with me your thoughts about the project?
Resister: I do not think the project is a good idea.
Project Manager: Why is that?
Resister: The new system will be slower than the current system.
Project Manager: I see. Why do you think the new system will be slower?
Resister: The most recent upgrade you put in place was slower. I assume this one will be slower, too.
Project Manager: How did the recent upgrade slow you down?
Resister: Our salespeople took 50 percent longer to complete transactions after the upgrade.
Project Manager: Is this the only reason for your concern?
Resister: Yes.
Project Manager: I understand. Thank you for sharing your concern. The new upgrade has fixed the time delays. I'll show you with the test version on my laptop . . .

Instead of making assumptions about the reason for the stakeholder's resistance, which is not a good idea, the project manager asked questions and listened. In this case, the project manager asked five questions and then was in a position to respond.

before executing the process of identifying rational/emotional/political resistance. By following these techniques in the proper order, the project manager has the highest probability of overcoming resistance.

The Five Why's   When there is resistance, the first step is to understand, as precisely as possible, why the resistance is occurring. Begin by asking at least five clarifying questions. After asking each question, listen carefully to the response. The goal is to determine the root cause(s) of the resistance. Sometimes the source of resistance is obvious and stated. In other cases the project manager must dig to find the source of the objection.

Asking why five times is a guideline. It reminds us that we are more likely to get to the source of resistance by asking many questions, not just one or two. Depending on the situation, a larger or smaller number of questions may be required.

At the conclusion of the five why's exercise the project manager may have the necessary information to respond and overcome the objection. If the project manager does not have enough information, or if his or her response does not yield support from the resistant stakeholder, then the project manager should move to the next step in the process for responding to resisters. The next step is to determine if the stakeholder is resisting for reasons that are rational, emotional, or political.

Rational/Emotional/Political   A framework passed down over time in the implementation consulting industry states that people tend to either resist or support change for three reasons: rational, emotional, and/or political. If the five why's do not work to gain stakeholder support, the next step is to assess whether the stakeholder is resisting for rational, emotional, or political reasons.

Rational   Rational stakeholders are those who resist due to honest disagreements on project facts and details. Perhaps they do not support the underlying assumptions in the analysis. Maybe they truly believe the new system will not work. For whatever reasons, rational resisters see the facts differently. With rational resisters, the best way to overcome the resistance is to have an open conversation about the facts. Show them the business case and assumptions. Listen to their feedback and determine if it has merit. The resistant stakeholder may be doing the project team a favor by identifying a flaw in the plan.

Open conversations about project facts and details are typically effective with rational resisters. This approach, however, is not likely to earn buy-in from an emotional or political resister. In fact, this approach may make the situation worse when dealing with an emotional or political resister.

Emotional   Emotional resisters are stakeholders who are upset about the project because they are personally sensitive to some aspect of it. Stakeholders can become emotional for any number of reasons, including:

- Disappointment about changes to an area of the organization that has sentimental value to them.
- Concern that some of their direct reports will be taken away.
- Frustration that a system or process they designed is being replaced by the project with something new.
- Anger that their voices are not being heard.
- Fear that the project will take resources away from their personal pet project(s).

Attempting to overcome emotional resistance with facts is counterproductive. Instead, project managers should respond to emotional resisters the same way they might respond to people going through a difficult time in their lives. This requires sensitivity, listening, and being nonjudgmental.

Talk to emotional resisters person to person, heart to heart. Listen to their stories. Hear about all of the hard work they put into the current system. Share a laugh. The stakeholders' resistance may turn into support once they understand that the project manager has empathy for their emotions.

Political   Political resisters oppose the project for concerns related to their standing in the organization, their department's standing, or some other issue related to perceived political winners and losers from the

Risks of Responding to Emotional Resistance with Rational Facts

Consider the example of an emotional resister who is opposing the implementation of a new company logo. The resister, a member the marketing department, designed the current logo and spent months getting everyone's support for it. All of this was years ago, but the logo is still of great significance to the resister.

The project manager realizes this individual is a resister but fails to recognize that the resistance is emotional. Instead of responding to the emotions, the project manager meets with the resister and shares the business case for the new company logo. The project manager, in great detail, lays out how the current logo, the one the resister designed, is outdated and ineffective.

The project manager then shares the business case that compares the current logo to the new one by describing all of the faults with the current logo and the benefits of the new one. The resister grows increasingly frustrated with the conversation. The project manager is outlining the faults in the current logo, *his* logo, and all the benefits in the new logo, the *project manager's* logo. The resister vows to fight even harder to block the new design.

In this situation, the project manager has made the problem worse by attempting to overcome emotional resistance with a rational argument. A savvy project manager would ask the five why's and uncover as much information as possible about the resistant stakeholder's goals and motives prior to responding.

project. The resistance may be for personal reasons. Alternatively, the stakeholder's resistance may be on behalf of a group the resistant stakeholder is leading or perceives himself or herself to be leading. Political resisters might not have an opinion on the facts and might not be emotional.

Facilitate Through Politics—Don't Play Politics

A global webinar on the topic of buy-in was conducted in August 2012. In the question-and-answer period, several attendees asked questions about dealing with project politics. It is a real issue for project managers.

There is no one best answer on how to deal with project politics. Politics is a way to make decisions and resolve competing interests. The savvy project manager observes the political forces at play and then charts a course to respond effectively and appropriately without personally getting in the middle of the conflict. When political forces are present, it may be an excellent time for the project manager to involve the executive sponsor. Senior executives are often skilled and experienced at navigating organizational politics.

Political behavior is found in all levels of an organization. Politics is a real part of the project environment and shapes project outcomes. The project manager is encouraged to remain aware of political behavior and troubleshoot how it impacts the project. Smart project managers call on their awareness, ability to make Whole Body Decisions™, adaptability, and diplomacy to guide them to the right answer.

Hybrid Approaches Resister behavior does not always fit neatly into one of the three categories of rational, emotional, or political. Hybrid behavior is quite common where a stakeholder exhibits characteristics of two or three of the categories. In this case, the project manager may need several meetings to identify and work through the stakeholder's resistance one issue at a time.

Do Not Push So Hard If none of the techniques presented here have worked, a final technique is to back off for a period of time. When a new idea enters our consciousness, it takes time to process it. While people are processing information, it is counterproductive for the project manager to continue pushing. The individuals may reflexively resist while they give themselves time to think about the new idea or concept.

Think of the image of the hourglass or spinning circle on a computer screen when the computer's memory is processing something.

Hybrid Resistance

A project has been launched to merge two customer service groups into a single group. Each group currently has a dedicated director. One of the directors is very concerned about the change. The director is concerned for rational, emotional, and political reasons:

- *Rational*. Each customer service group currently serves a different product offering. The director is concerned that merging the groups will reduce the product-specific knowledge and the pride of ownership currently present in the group.
- *Emotional*. The director created the group out of nothing 10 years ago. He is saddened that the group might be absorbed by a large, combined group where it would lose its identity.
- *Political*. The director is junior to the leader of the other group. The director is concerned that the leader of the other group will take over the combined group, relegating him to a less powerful role.

Using the techniques discussed in this chapter, the project manager should work through the rational, emotional, and political issues separately. Each type of issue requires a different approach.

In the case of the computer, the hourglass means: "Do not bother me. I am still processing what you asked me to do a few moments ago." It is the same idea with people. When people are processing, they often have a blank expression on their faces. When the project manager sees a blank look, it could be an indication that it is time to back off. It may be appropriate to stop the meeting or presentation.

When people emerge from the processing mode, they may have questions for the project manager. Depending on the magnitude of the change, it may take days or even weeks for them to fully process the change. If project managers continue the presentation despite receiving the blank look, they are wasting their own time and the other people's, too. If the project manager prepared all of the presentation, then it has the project manager's words, charts, and logic flow. The other people's brains may work in very different ways. They may need time to process what they are seeing and hearing.

Resistant stakeholders may want clarification. The successful project manager allows them to process the information on their own terms, not on the project team's terms. Everyone processes information differently. It is a good sign if they are engaged and actively trying to learn. This is the project manager's opening to get buy-in.

It is important to note that what the project team might consider a very small change someone else may view as dramatic. The project team works with the changes on a daily basis and has plenty of time to think about the changes, shape them, and ultimately accept them. The resistant stakeholder may be hearing about the changes for the first time. Imagine taking everything that has been done in a project over a period of months and sharing it all with someone in several minutes. It is easy to see why many stakeholders require time to process all of the information.

People do not process change on schedule with the project plan. The project plan has deadlines and deliverables. Project plan time lines are created from the amount of time required to complete work packages. Project plans are not created from the amount of time it takes for stakeholders to process the change.

The project plan might dictate that a new system needs to be in place in two weeks, yet it might require three months of effort to earn the appropriate stakeholder buy-in. The savvy project manager builds enough time into project plans for people to process change. Reconciling project plans with sufficient time for stakeholder buy-in is part of the art and science of project management.

Balancing the art and science of human change is difficult. Project success is achieved by focusing on the Balanced Approach discussed in Chapter 1. Effective project managers use technical skills, business acumen, and Sixth Sense people skills together in harmony to navigate the conflicts between how people process change and the time lines and other constraints placed on that change. This is real-world project management.

See Chapter 1, What Is a Stakeholder?, for more detail on the Balanced Approach.

Negotiate If the steps presented here have not worked, it is time to negotiate. Negotiation is a two-way street, so project managers may need to cede one or more of their positions for successful negotiation. Stakeholder negotiation is the topic of the next chapter.

Summary

Earning buy-in is an iterative process, not a single event. In this chapter we discussed a three-step process for earning buy-in: include, observe, and respond. The include section discussed the importance of inviting project stakeholders to be part of the project process. Stakeholders are more likely to support what they are part of. In the observe section we discussed how to become more in tune with the verbal and nonverbal cues project stakeholders display. Overall awareness helps the project manager know how to respond. Finally, we talked about how to respond to the project stakeholder concerns. The project manager must have several different skills to earn support. The successful project manager continues to use the Circle of Support even after support has been awarded.

Project managers should avoid the reflex of responding immediately to all stakeholder criticisms or concerns. Note that the respond section is third and not first. Responding comes only after the project manager has included and observed. The proper response varies by individual and by situation, so the project manager must include and observe stakeholders to determine the best way to respond.

The next chapter, on negotiation, discusses how to arrive at an agreeable conclusion if buy-in is not achieved. Learning the Circle of Support and its subcomponents is easy. Mastering them takes a lifetime.

Chapter Twelve

Negotiation

If you come to a negotiation table saying you have the final truth, that you know nothing but the truth and that is final, you will get nothing.

Harri Holkeri

his chapter focuses on negotiation skills for project managers. Project managers frequently negotiate over project resources, project scope, budget allocations, and many other items related to their projects. Also, the dynamic nature of projects requires ongoing negotiations; projects are about change, and change is not always agreed to by all stakeholders.

We discuss 10 tips for successful negotiations in the project environment. The tips address when to negotiate, how to negotiate, and techniques to turn power plays (which the project manager cannot control) into negotiations (which the project manager has some control over). Used together, these tips will help project managers greatly improve their chances of success in negotiation.

Negotiation Is a Two-Way Street

Negotiaiton is broadly defined as an agreement reached between two or more parties that compromise. Synonyms include cooperation, concession, and diplomacy. These synonyms suggest that negotiation means working together and mutual give-and-take. According to this definition, negotiation is *not* forcing a stakeholder to conform to our way of thinking or having other stakeholders force their will over us. This is a power play.

Project Manager as Negotiator

Projects create change. Change is often controversial. Stakeholders might disagree on project scope, budget, time line, or any number of other variables. The project manager who chooses to ignore all of these disagreements is likely to have a lower project success rate than project managers who embrace the conflict as part of their role. Successful project managers hone their negotiation skills and help the organization work through the inevitable disagreements.

It is important for the project manager to understand the difference between a negotiation and a power play. In a negotiation, the project manager has a chance of changing the other party's perspective. In a negotiation, the project manager can engage in a conversation and work collaboratively toward results. In a power play, by contrast, the project manager is not able to do either of these.

When project managers force their will on a stakeholder, then this is a power play too. Project managers are not encouraged to deploy power plays even when it's an option to do so. Project managers, by definition, are leaders of change. Project changes are more sustainable when they are created collaboratively with stakeholders and not forced on stakeholders. Consider the example of a pendulum. If the pendulum is held at an angle, it stays in the same position as long as it's held there. As soon as the force holding it is removed, the pendulum swings back down.

People behave in a similar manner. When the project team holds everyone in a certain position, they may stay there due to the force of organizational pressure being placed on them. However, this is not sustainable change. Once the force of the project team is removed, the people are likely to swing back to prior behaviors. A misunderstanding of this fundamental reality has derailed many projects. Power plays are discussed in more detail in the next part of this chapter.

Ten Tips for Negotiations in Projects

In this section we discuss 10 tips for successfully negotiating in projects. Although these tips may apply to any negotiation situation, including those outside of project management, the tips are specifically intended for projects.

Negotiation Tip #1: Shift Power Plays into Negotiations

Project managers may find themselves in situations where influential stakeholders force their will on them or on the project. This is a power play. Any situation where the project manager is at the receiving end of some direction that the project manager has no control over, no ability to discuss, and no ability to negotiate is a power play.

When subject to a power play, the project manager's goal is to shift the power play into a negotiation. If project managers can shift the power play into a negotiation, then they have a better chance of influencing the final outcome. The project manager is the less powerful stakeholder in a power play, so it is not recommended that the project manager attempt to fight the power play with his or her own show of power. In this situation the project manager is not likely to be successful.

Instead, the primary tactic a project manager can deploy to convert a power play into a negotiation is to help the stakeholder understand the consequences of their position. This technique is discussed next.

Power Play

The executive vice president of a consumer products company wants to increase the sales of a new line of products she recently championed. The sales have been slow since the new line was launched six months earlier. She reviews several options and decides the best way to increase sales is to create a new section in the company's online store that highlights the product line's features and benefits.

She does some research and discovers there is currently a project underway to redesign the web store. The project is focused on improving the look and feel of individual store pages. Although her decision for the online store is outside of the scope of work for this project, the executive vice president meets with the team and tells them they must create the new section she desires. She tells the team there is no room for negotiation.

This is a power play.

Helping Stakeholders Understand Consequences

In a power play, one or more project stakeholders attempt to force their will on the project manager and the project team. Saying no may lead to further conflict. Also, saying no can have negative consequences for the project manager from a relationship standpoint and potentially from a career standpoint. Instead, the project manager should help the stakeholders understand the consequences of their decision.

The project manager should approach the stakeholders with open-ended questions in response to their power play. Open-ended questions are a diplomatic way to help the stakeholders deepen their thinking around the controversial viewpoint. With open-ended questions, the project manager can subtly challenge the stakeholders' thinking without telling them they are incorrect.

Using Open-Ended Questions to Change Attitudes

Jorge, the vice president of operations, would like the line expansion project to be completed one month earlier. Cindy is the project manager on this important project to increase the capacity of manufacturing operations by adding a second manufacturing line. Cindy knows that accelerating the project by one month will be very expensive. She does not, however, want to be seen as confrontational and decides to schedule a meeting with her boss, Jorge, to discuss the project acceleration.

Jorge (vice president of operations): Hi, Cindy. How are you?

Cindy (project manager): Just fine. Thanks for meeting with me today.

Jorge: No problem. What's up?

Cindy: I wanted to talk with you about accelerating the line expansion.

Jorge: Great. That's very important to me.

Cindy: Can you explain why the acceleration is so important?

Jorge: Sure. If we get the production line up one month faster, then we can secure a one-time project from a client in Brazil. This project will lead to $50,000 in profit.

Cindy: I see. Do you think we should compare the value of that profit against the additional costs to get the line completed early?

Jorge: That makes sense. But I did not realize there would be additional costs to completing the line early.

Cindy: Unfortunately, there will be additional costs. The contractors are currently staffing the project at two people per week. To complete the project early, they need to double their staffing to four people per week. They don't have any more of their regular resources available so they will need to subcontract the work. The estimated additional cost of the two resources is $150,000.

Jorge: That's expensive.

Cindy: Yes. Well, what do you think we should do? Is the new contract in Brazil worth an additional $150,000 in project costs?

Jorge: Upon further reflection of this information, no. Let's keep the project on its current schedule. I'll see if there's any chance we can do the Brazil work one month later. Thanks for your help.

Using this approach Cindy let the facts speak for her. Jorge appreciated her candor. She is not viewed as an obstructionist or a barrier to Jorge's wishes. In fact, just the opposite: Cindy is seen as a problem solver and an individual who is helping the stakeholder understand the trade-offs of his decisions. When in a power play, ask open-ended questions to help the stakeholder understand the ramifications of the decision. Then, just as Cindy did, ask the stakeholder to make the decision based on the more complete information.

Saying Yes When We Really Mean No

If the open-ended questioning approach does not work, there may be situations where the project manager's only choice is to say no. This is difficult to do. In fact, in many cases, in particular as the result of power plays, project managers say yes when they know they can't deliver what is being asked of them. Increasingly, project managers and other professionals find themselves in the position where they accept work they are not able to complete. This puts everyone in an uncomfortable situation.

If the project manager has accepted work that cannot be completed, it is best to acknowledge this as early as possible. Acknowledgment might involve a frank conversation with the relevant stakeholder and an explanation of the constraints preventing the project manager from honoring the request. The project manager should highlight trade-offs, options, and alternatives to position himself or herself as a problem solver.

Saying No Diplomatically

The *New York Times* printed an article on January 14, 2012, titled "When You're the Worker Who Can't Say No." The article ran in the "Career Couch" column.

The author of this book was quoted in this article and called on experiences managing projects to share perspectives on how to say no diplomatically. An excerpt from the article follows:

> If you think you may already have more work than you can handle, tell your boss that, because you're juggling other time-sensitive projects, you need to examine the details of this new task to determine if there's some way you can fit it in, Mr. Roeder says. You may find that you won't be able to, but automatically responding "no" without any consideration gives the impression you don't want to deal with it, he says. "And you don't want to be known as the person who always says no unless they get the perfect assignment," he adds.

Negotiation Tip #2: Do the Homework

Effective negotiators do their homework before, during, and even after negotiations.

Homework before the Negotiation

Homework done before negotiations is crucial to prepare for success. Questions that effective negotiators ask themselves might include:

- Am I negotiating with an individual or a group?
- If I am negotiating with a group, who within the group is expected to have the most influence over the final outcome?

Prepare for Success Prior to Beginning Negotiations

Sun Tzu's *The Art of War*, written thousands of years ago, is an influential book on military strategy. Many of the book's lessons can be applied to other areas, too. In his book Sun Tzu highlights the importance of preparations in the following quote:

> A victorious army first wins and then seeks battle; a defeated army first battles and then seeks victory.

SOURCE: Sun Tzu, *The Art of War*, Shambhala Publications, 1991 translated by Thomas Cleary, page 29.

- What is the other party likely to want out of the negotiation?
- Of the different items the other party wants, which ones are likely to be the most important?
- What is the style of the individual(s) being negotiated with? For example, do they have a reputation for being collaborative or secretive, sharing with information throughout the process or withholding of information until the final stages of negotiation?
- Who do I need approval from before entering into a final agreement?
- What topics are important to my project? Which ones are the most important if I can't get everything?
- How much time is there to complete this negotiation?
- What resources are available to help me with the negotiation?
- What resources do the other parties have to help them with negotiation?
- Is there data available that supports my positions? How can I get access to that data?
- Is there data available that supports the other parties' positions? How might I respond if they bring their data into the negotiations?

- What big-picture issues are happening that might impact the negotiation? For example:
  - Does the macroeconomic situation impact these negotiations?
  - Are there other current events that could make a difference in this negotiation?
  - Are any of the parties involved in the negotiation working for organizations that are going through an organizational change that might impact the negotiation?

Homework done before negotiations can pay significant dividends during negotiations. It is best not to be surprised during the negotiation. Extra time spent doing homework means a lower probability that data, people, or changes arise during the negotiation that surprise the negotiator.

Homework during Negotiations

Expert negotiators continue to do their homework during the negotiation. As the other party brings up new pieces of information, effective negotiators avoid commenting on the new information until they have had a chance to research it. Between discussions, the effective negotiator looks into the new information and determines its credibility. The effective negotiator also continues to seek an understanding of the individuals he or she is negotiating with and their positions. It is common for new information to be revealed throughout the course of a negotiation. The negotiator does not take this new information at face value, but instead does homework to dig into the information, validate it, and understand it deeply.

Homework after the Negotiation

There may be situations where the effective negotiator continues to do homework after the formal negotiation is complete. One situation where this occurs is an ongoing partnership. There may be a negotiation today to initiate the partnership. Today's negotiation, however, may need to be repeated every year. As soon as today's negotiation is

Are Things as They Appear?

A project has just been launched to fix the improper installation of a new enterprise-wide system for customer relationship management (CRM). The new CRM system has been broadly blamed for many operational problems, including poor performance at the company's call center. In the call center, customer hold times are currently over 50 minutes. Most customers hang up before the agent gets to their call. Customers who wait are irate about the long hold times.

The project manager schedules a meeting with the lead of the CRM implementation to negotiate the time line for call center system improvements. The project manager expects a difficult conversation. In preparation for the meeting, the project manager conducts extensive homework into the call center delays and the root causes of the delays, and discovers that none of the agents were properly trained on how to use the new CRM system.

Instead of focusing the negotiation on how to fix the system itself, the project manager decides to focus on how to train those who are using the system. The project manager's homework has paid off, and the organization is now one step closer to a successful project outcome.

complete, it may be in the best interest of the negotiator to begin doing homework and planning for next year's negotiation.

Monitoring compliance with negotiated agreements is another situation where homework is required after the negotiation is completed. The effective negotiator ensures that the other party is compliant with the various commitments. Depending on the nature of the negotiation, there are different ways to monitor compliance. In some cases, self-reporting may be a sufficient form of compliance. In other cases, there may be a need for a third party to validate compliance.

Negotiation Tip #3: Be Aware of Others

Effective negotiators have a keen awareness of other stakeholders. Awareness is a common thread through all project stakeholder management skills discussed in this book. For example, the project manager should use awareness in identifying stakeholders, when getting buy-in from stakeholders, and when negotiating. There is no one best way to negotiate. Awareness informs the project manager about the reality of the current situation. Armed with this awareness and with the skills discussed in this book, the project manager can decide on the best course of action.

Awareness of Verbal and Nonverbal Cues

Awareness requires paying attention to both verbal and nonverbal behavior. The project manager should pay particular attention to the consistency, or lack thereof, in the verbal and nonverbal messaging. For example, stakeholders who say they support the project but glare as they are saying it might be demonstrating inconsistent verbal and nonverbal behavior. This does not necessarily indicate disagreement but should be noted for further homework.

Also, project managers should pay attention to consistency in their own verbal and nonverbal messaging. For example, the project manager smiles when delivering good messages and has a serious expression when delivering difficult news. Matching verbal and nonverbal behavior can require considerable training. However, it's important because others are likely to perceive the project manager's level of authenticity by the consistency of verbal and nonverbal messaging.

Negotiation Tip #4: Separate Relationships from Opinions

The project manager's relationship with a stakeholder does not necessarily direct that stakeholder's opinion, or position, in the negotiation. Said differently, if the project manager has a good relationship with a stakeholder, that does not mean the stakeholder will agree with the project manager. Also, if the project manager has a poor relationship with a stakeholder, that does not mean the stakeholder will disagree with the project manager.

Separating relationships from opinions is important. A project managers' judgment becomes clouded if they confuse friends with people who agree with everything they are pushing for in their projects. This may seem self-evident, yet it is common for project managers to experience frustration when people they thought were their friends disagree with them.

Each person in a negotiation is likely to have some sort of position or opinion. There are actions that each party wants and also likely actions that each party prefers to avoid. The effective negotiator respects these positions. Project managers should not allow their opinion on a stakeholder's personality to influence their understanding of the stakeholder's position.

Relationships Are Not a Free Pass

Two engineering groups are being merged into a single group. One of the legacy engineering groups is in North America and the other is in Europe. The heads of the two groups have a deep personal relationship that goes back 20 years. They attended the weddings of each other's children, worked collaboratively to implement bold new strategies in their organizations, and met several times a year for friendly conversations over dinner.

The head of the European group is selected as the new leader of the combined organization. He knows the merger will be a lot of work. However, one thing he is not concerned about is working with his counterpart in North America. After all, he thinks to himself, they have a deep personal relationship.

However, when the details begin to emerge, the North American counterpart resists the change. Despite the personal friendship, his career aspirations and desire to support his team trump the personal relationship. The personal relationship begins to suffer as the conflict flares.

Reflecting on the lessons of this story, the project manager learns not to take a relationship for granted. Relationships can assist with the implementation of change but do not guarantee agreement. Negotiation skills are still needed.

Negotiation Tip #5: Clearly Communicate the Project Needs

The project manager should clearly communicate specific requests. Less experienced project managers may be inclined to withhold most details. This is a mistake. The project manager should be direct and open. Direct and open communication is more likely to yield the desired results, particularly when the other party reciprocates. Other stakeholders can only react to what they know. If they are not aware of the project needs, then they are not able to help even if they want to.

Using Multiple Communications Channels

The project manager should use multiple communication channels to share the project needs. For example, an e-mail might be sent to key stakeholders expressing the project requirements. This e-mail might be followed by meetings, which then might be followed up with a simple chart or graph that explains what was discussed. In this example, the project manager is using written, verbal, and visual communication to help ensure that the message is understood.

Using multiple communication channels is more likely to get the message through. Different people process messages in different ways. The project manager who relies only on e-mail may miss an opportunity to clearly communicate the project needs to an entire section of stakeholders who are more likely to understand information if it's communicated verbally.

See Chapter 7, Stakeholder Communication, for more detail on how to communicate across different channels.

Negotiation Tip #6: Know Your BATNA

Getting to Yes, by Roger Fisher and William Uri, appeared in 1981 and is one of the most influential books on negotiation. *Getting to Yes* focuses on how to achieve win–win situations in negotiations. One of the main concepts discussed in this book is the "Best Alternative To a Negotiated Agreement" (BATNA).

Understanding Your BATNA

The negotiator's BATNA is the best course of action available to the negotiator if negotiations fall apart. Negotiators should review the choices they expect to have if the negotiation fails and determine which of these choices is the best option. This is their BATNA. The BATNA is used to help the negotiator understand the risks and rewards of negotiating.

If the negotiator's BATNA is better than the expected negotiated outcome, then the negotiator is not likely to be highly motivated to enter into a negotiated agreement. If the negotiator's BATNA is worse than the expected negotiated outcome, however, then the negotiator is motivated to achieve a negotiated agreement. The BATNA helps negotiators determine how important a negotiated outcome is to them.

BATNA

A project manager is negotiating for additional time to be added to the project deadline. The project manager requests four more weeks to complete the project.

The project manager is requesting additional time because one of the key project resources was recently redeployed to another project. The resource is the only in-house expert on human resources policies. The project manager is asking for an extension to allow the expert resource to work on the other project and then return to his project.

If additional time is not granted, the second-best option is to bring in an outside expert. This costs additional money. All of the other options, such as killing the project, are less desirable than bringing in the outside resource. Therefore, bringing in an outside resource is the project manager's best alternative to a negotiated agreement (BATNA), but this BATNA is not better than the negotiated outcome being sought, an extension.

In addition to understanding the overall BATNA, it is also important to understand the BATNA for each subcomponent of the negotiation. For example, a negotiation might involve a price, a time line, and the scope of work. If the project manager is working with a tight budget, the BATNA for a cost that is over budget might be very poor. The project might not be able to be completed if the cost is higher than the budget. The project manager, however, might have more flexibility on the schedule. In this case the project manager's BATNA for an extended time line might be fairly attractive.

Negotiation Tip #7: When in Multiparty Negotiations, Align Interests

There are two types of negotiations: single-party and multiparty. In a single-party negotiation, the project manager negotiates with one individual or group. In a multiparty negotiation, the project manager is negotiating with two or more individuals or groups. Each type of negotiation has advantages and disadvantages. (See Table 12.1.)

Single-Party Negotiations

In single-party negotiations, the project manager needs to understand the position of only one person or group. This does not necessarily make the negotiation easier. However, it reduces the complexity when

Table 12.1 Types of Negotiations

	Single-Party	Multi-party
Advantages	Less complex May be easier to build trust and rapport	Possible to gain the strength of a coalition Potential for additional paths to success if one or two parties are resistant
Disadvantages	Lacks strength that can come with coalitions More difficult to break a logjam if the other party is not willing to change their position	More complex Difficult to align various interests

compared to multiparty negotiation. One disadvantage of the single-party negotiation is that the project manager might lose the benefits that come from building a coalition.

Multiparty Negotiations

In multiparty negotiations, the project manager must deal with multiple people or groups. This creates more complexity in the negotiation. There is likely to be a broader range of interests, many of which are not aligned. In a multiparty negotiation, the project manager should seek the individuals and groups that have interests aligned with his or her own. A coalition can be formed around common interests. It is important to note that most individuals or groups are unlikely to agree with the project manager on every single issue. The project manager should highlight those issues that are agreed on and use them as a central point for discussions.

Negotiation Tip #8: Build Coalitions, and Watch for Others' Coalitions

When in multiparty negotiations, project managers should try to build coalitions. This is important because the project manager does not typically have position authority. Therefore, project managers can greatly strengthen their position by aligning themselves with others who do have position authority.

Coalition building can be a very powerful technique for the project manager to move the project forward. It is also an influential way for adversaries to trump the project manager. Savvy project managers, while building their own coalition, regularly scan the negotiation environment to identify other coalitions that may be forming against them.

Definition of a Coalition

A coalition is created when two or more parties agree to work together toward a common goal. Coalitions may form in multiparty negotiations. There are advantages and disadvantages to building a coalition.

Advantages of coalitions include:

- Expand the project manager's influence.
- Increase the resource pool.
- Broaden the reach of the project message.

Disadvantages of coalitions include:

- The project manager's scarce time and effort may be required to hold the coalition together.
- Stakeholder interests within the coalition may not always be aligned.
- Infighting within the coalition can harm the project.

Strengthening Coalitions

Project managers can strengthen their coalitions by making the value of joining clear. For example, the savvy project manager clearly articulates to potential coalition partners what the partner can gain by being a part of the coalition. Project managers further strengthen coalitions by making the costs of not joining equally clear. For example, the project manager might explain that potential partners will have less opportunity to shape the scope of the project if they are not part of the coalition.

It is important to recognize that others will attempt to build their own coalitions. Similar to a game of chess, project managers must simultaneously assess their position and the position of their adversaries. This requires vigilantly keeping an eye on their own coalition while also keeping an eye on coalitions that may be forming that could jeopardize their chances of project success.

Once a coalition has been formed, the project manager must continue to nurture relationships to keep the coalition together. It is not uncommon for coalitions to fall apart as the project advances.

Breaks in Coalitions

Coalitions are often fragile and can be easily broken. Here is a partial list of items that could cause breaks in a coalition:

- One of the key stakeholders in the coalition leaves the project.
- A new group is added to the coalition and attempts to shift the coalition closer to their own perspective.
- A new project manager is assigned to the project.
- New information arises.

- Changes in the project environment occur such as an announcement of organizational changes within any of the stakeholder organizations.
- One or more coalition partners change their minds and attempt to renegotiate the coalition objectives to create a better perceived advantage for themselves.

Effective project managers look for signs that indicate their coalition may be splintering. Any identified cracks should be quickly and proactively addressed.

Negotiation Tip #9: Logic Does Not Always Win Negotiations

Traditionally, the discipline of project management has been grounded in analytical and logical charts, graphs, templates, and tools. The history of project management is replete with spreadsheets, software tools with definite deliverables and dates, and other analytical tools. Although these tools are helpful, projects do not always progress in a straight line. This is a critical point for project managers to keep at the front of their minds when engaging in negotiations. Their logic, regardless of how solid it might be, may not win the negotiation.

Uncovering Hidden Emotions

Stakeholders tend to resist change for three reasons: rational, emotional, and/or political. We discussed that logic may not win because others can have different logic. Another reason why logic might not win is because the stakeholder is focused on emotions or politics. Some people may use logic as a front for their emotional positions that may be more difficult to justify than logical concerns would be. The project manager successful at uncovering emotional and political interests is more likely to prevail in negotiations.

Another reason why logic does not always win negotiations is because there are also emotions and politics involved in negotiations.

See Chapter 11, Buy-In, for more discussion on rational, emotional, and political behavior.

Negotiation Tip #10: End the Negotiation If Necessary

The project manager must make decisions on when to negotiate and when to walk away from the negotiation. Although negotiating with project stakeholders is typically the best answer, there are some situations where it is in the project manager's best interest not to negotiate. The following guidelines help the project manager determine if it is better to continue negotiations or to end the negotiations.

Logic Does Not Always Win Negotiations

An engineering team is designing a new printing press. The project requirements call for a press that is fast and reliable. The lead engineer completes a detailed cost-benefit analysis and determines that the total expense can be reduced by 25 percent if a motor is used that is slightly less powerful. With the less powerful motor, operating speeds will be 5 percent slower. The lead engineer reasons that this is a good trade-off.

In the project report-out meeting, the lead engineer provides his analysis and shows how he has identified a 25 percent cost reduction for a printing press that is 5 percent slower. He presents the logical details in an organized and structured format. The director of design does not support the argument. She argues that speed is the most important issue. Customers are willing to pay for speed, and a 25 percent cost premium, the director of design argues, can be justified by many of their customers by the 5 percent increase in speed.

The lead engineer becomes agitated. He does not agree. He personally would not pay 25 percent more for a 5 percent increase in speed. His logic is different from the design director's. In this case, both the lead engineer and the director of design may be making completely logical arguments. The director of design, however, has the authority to make the decision and prevails. The lead engineer's logic has not won the negotiation.

Do *Not* Negotiate When the BATNA Is Better Than a Negotiated Agreement

There may be some cases in which the project manager does not want to negotiate because it diminishes the outcome. For example, it does not make sense for the project manager to negotiate a new price with a vendor that has already agreed to a higher price that can be enforced. The best alternative to the new price is the higher price contractually agreed to.

Do *Not* Negotiate When Ethics, Legal, or Regulatory Requirements Are Compromised

Legal and ethical requirements, of course, should not be compromised during negotiations. As part of the negotiation homework, the project manager should research ethical, legal, and regulatory issues that may arise during negotiations.

Do Negotiate When the BATNA Is Poor

A poor BATNA, by definition, means the project manager has much to benefit from negotiating. Note that BATNAs may change over the course of negotiations. Savvy project managers regularly update their homework to determine if their options, and BATNA, have changed.

Do Negotiate for the Greater Good

Project management is not a straight line. There are times when project managers must negotiate with stakeholders to keep the project moving forward even if it means keeping the project moving forward in a suboptimal manner. For example, a key stakeholder may have the desire to add to the project scope. The project manager may understand that the additional scope will lengthen the project time line. Even though the project manager does not want the time line to lengthen, it may be in the best interest of the project manager to negotiate with the stakeholder and accept the additional scope of work. This is the sort of daily decision making that project managers must do to navigate the real-world environment their projects operate in.

Summary

In summary, negotiation is a critical skill for project managers. Project managers negotiate everything from resources to project scope to project time lines. Outcomes of these negotiations add up to a series of agreements, decisions, and actions that impact project success.

In this chapter, we discussed 10 tips for negotiation success. These tips should be practiced on an ongoing basis to improve confidence and performance:

Negotiation Tip #1: Shift Power Plays into Negotiations
Negotiation Tip #2: Do the Homework
Negotiation Tip #3: Be Aware of Others
Negotiation Tip #4: Separate Relationships from Opinions
Negotiation Tip #5: Clearly Communicate the Project Needs
Negotiation Tip #6: Know Your BATNA
Negotiation Tip #7: When in Multiparty Negotiations, Align Interests
Negotiation Tip #8: Build Coalitions, and Watch for Others' Coalitions
Negotiation Tip #9: Logic Does Not Always Win Negotiations
Negotiation Tip #10: End the Negotiation If Necessary

Confidence is critical in negotiations. Confidence is an intangible skill that often determines the difference between success and failure. Most stakeholders can sense confidence in the project manager and are less likely to fight a confident project manager than one they perceive to be indecisive or uncertain.

It is also important to note that negotiations are dynamic and circumstances often change during the course of a negotiation. Project managers must constantly keep themselves aware of changes in the positions of their stakeholders. When changes are detected, the wise project manager quickly addresses the changes and keeps the project moving forward.

References

Brox, Denene. 2011. "Power of Persuasion." *PM Network*, December.

Fisher, Roger, and William Ury. 1981; 2nd ed. with Bruce Patton, 1991. *Getting to Yes*. Boston: Houghton Mifflin.

PMBOK® Guide, 5th ed. 2013. Newtown Square, PA: Project Management Institute.

Roeder, Tres. 2011. *A Sixth Sense for Project Management*. Bloomington, IN: AuthorHouse.

Roeder Consulting webinar survey data, 2010 and 2012.

Zimmerman, Eileen. 2012. "When You're the Worker Who Can't Say No." *New York Times*, January 14.

About the Author

Tres Roeder is a recognized global expert on project management and organizational change. He has been quoted by the *New York Times*, the *Wall Street Journal*, *MSN Money*, Microsoft Press, Inc.com, the Project Management Institute, *Crain's Cleveland Business*, and the *Cleveland Plain Dealer*, to name a few. Mr. Roeder founded Roeder Consulting in 2001 after serving as a consultant with Booz Allen Hamilton. He has worked with many of the world's top brands, including Toyota, John Deere, HSBC, Chrysler, ADM, the Scotts Miracle-Gro Company, and American Greetings.

Mr. Roeder's best-selling first book, *A Sixth Sense for Project Management*, details how to achieve project success by deploying a balanced approach with a particular emphasis on people. A member of the National Speakers Association, Mr. Roeder regularly speaks at global events, including the Project Management Institute's Global Congresses, where he once received a coveted encore presentation.

Mr. Roeder is a Project Management Professional (PMP®). He holds a BA in economics from the University of Illinois and an MBA from the Kellogg Graduate School of Management at Northwestern University.

Index